喆哲嚞 埑悊晢折

形聲字。從口，折聲。

本義：聰明，有智慧。
哲，知也。《說文》
哲，智也。《爾雅》
濬哲文明，溫恭允塞。《虞書·舜典》
哲夫成城，哲婦傾城。《詩經·大雅·瞻卬》
視之不明，是謂不哲。《後漢紀·桓帝紀》

跨越時空的覺知

覺知

克里希納穆提◎著
KRISHNAMURTI

克氏首度公開發表的演講錄

陳召強◎譯

目 錄
Contents

獨具一格的生活方式

　　我們是否有時感覺自己在浪費生命，覺得生命毫無意義，而外在環境和內心世界又都充滿了衝突與困惑？在這本演講集（本書收錄了克里希那穆提在加利福尼亞、英格蘭、印度和瑞士的公開演講內容，其中大部分為首次公開發表）中，克里希那穆提就此進行思考，並提出了一種截然不同、獨具一格的生活方式——無拘無束、安寧平和。

　　他指出，如果我們能清楚瞭解自己的行動與反應模式以及與他人的關係，那麼生活將會變得無限美好且意義非凡。人類雖具有極高的心智，但卻習慣用它來解決問題，這實際上背離了自由的初衷。克里希那穆提解釋說，在認識自我時，我們要拒絕心理權威，以便讓自己的觀察和行動更為有效。如果我們的觀察擺脫了語言和思想的束縛，那麼自由與愛、美與善就會融為一體。

　　克里希那穆提談到，所謂生活的藝術是指生命中沒有任何的衝突，一個人完全免於恐懼，這其中也包括對死亡的恐懼。恐懼的根源、悲傷的原因，皆源於我們自身，而思想乃是時間和記憶與直接感知相互作用的一個過程。

　　只有學習傾聽、觀察、學習的藝術，才能真正理解到底是什麼在妨礙意識乃至生命的秩序。

　　對於以上種種，克里希那穆提皆以簡潔明瞭的語言賦予全新的解讀。

　　這些演講──克里希那穆提將其描述為我們與他之間的對話──發人深思，令人頓生感悟。透過這些論述，我們可以從中一窺神聖而永恆的空性。

雷・麥科伊

第一章 ┃ 生活就在當下

生活就發生在當下，
而非你的想像之中。
因此，
你現在邁出的第一步才是重要的。
如果第一步方向正確，
那麼整個生命之門就會向你敞開。

最偉大的藝術是生活的藝術，它比人類所能想像或創造的任何事物乃至所有的經典及諸神都要偉大。只有通過生活的藝術才能夠催生新的文化。而這種藝術只能源于全然的自由。

全然的自由並非理想，亦非終究要發生的事，而邁向自由的第一步亦是最後一步。但最重要的總是第一步，而非最後一步。你現在所做的事遠比將來某個時刻要做的事重要。生活就發生在當下，而非在你的想像之中。因此，你現在邁出的第一步才是重要的。如果第一步的方向正確，那麼整個生命之門就會向你敞開。這個正確的方向並非朝向一個理想或某個預設目標，而是與當下正在發生的事情密切相連。

我所介紹的不是什麼哲學理論體系，而是要指出「哲學」這個詞的本義——追求真理，熱愛生命。你在大學裡可學不到這些。我們是要在日常生活中學習生活的藝術。

生命的複雜之處就在於，我們很難從中挑出某件事情，並判斷它才是最重要的。如果要去選擇或區分哪件事最重要，會讓我們更加困惑。而且如果認爲某一方是最重要的，那麼生命中的其他方面就會被降至次要位置。實際上，我們要麼將整個生命的運動視爲一體，要麼挑出一個方面來涵蓋整個生命；前一種做法大多數人都極難做到，對於後一種做法，我們應當細加探究。

　　要探究可以涵蓋生命全部的面向，必須先摒棄所有的偏見、個人經驗以及先入爲主的觀念。同時，我們也要像優秀的科學家一樣，保持清醒的頭腦，不要爲過去積累的知識所左右，亦不可將情感加諸所觀察的事物之上。這是絕對必要的，否則，我們的探究過程就會深受恐懼、希冀和歡愉等情緒的影響。

　　學習生活的藝術是最重要的事情之一。那麼，有沒有一種生活方式可以徹底改變人生，從此沒有任何衝突與約束？這只有在全然活在當下時才可能找到。也就是說，只有仔細觀察當下正在發生的事，才能從中找到沒有衝突的生活方式。

　　這種觀察無關智慧，也不是情緒上的體驗，而是指敏銳、清楚、明晰地感知。這種感知不具有二元性或雙重性，其中亦不存在對立或矛盾。二元性源於事物的不完整，正是不完整性導致了對立，衝突也由此而生。但通過此種觀察，所感知的只有真理，別無其他。

心靈常會對當下發生的事件產生聯想與回應，這就會妨礙我們如實觀照。當下的事件不受時間的限制。「時間」這個概念本不存在，只不過是人類推斷出的產物；它是人類的遺產，也是找不到根源的負擔。帶著情緒去觀察，只會使我們被觀察的物件同化。若是在當下感到憤怒時，仔細觀察這種憤怒的情緒，你就會明瞭暴力背後的整個本質和結構。這種洞見，即是對所有暴力的終結。

憤怒的背後隱藏著很多故事。這些故事並不是孤立的，而是有著許多關聯。這些關聯，以及隨之而起的情緒，都會阻礙你如實觀照自己的憤怒。

觀察是如此簡單，以致你很容易忽略它。也就是說無論你正在做什麼事，比如行走、交談、冥想，當下所做之事皆可加以觀察。然而當我們那帶著情緒的心介入其中，觀察就會立即終結。因此，限定於當下的觀察無論何時都不會被曲解。

生活的藝術中並無記憶的安身之處。關係即生活的藝術。如果關係中存在記憶，那就不能稱為關係。關係存於人與人之間，而非他們的記憶之間。正是這些記憶將「你」和「我」區分開來，並製造了兩者的對立。因此無論如何，思想（亦即記憶）是不存在於關係中的。這就是生活的藝術。

世間萬物彼此聯結，從大自然中的飛鳥、岩石到白雲、星辰、藍天……我們周遭的所有事物都息息相關。沒有了關係，你就無法生活。然而，現今的人們生活在一個人際關係日漸淡漠的社會中，原本美好的關係已然遭到破壞。

　　只有當思想不曾玷污愛時，生活的藝術才能成眞。

第二章 | 思想是什麼

你是否發現內心深處其實除了
過去攝取的書本知識和對所處
社會的回饋之外一無所有？
而那一切，也不過是思想的創造。
但思想並不能代表人的所有身體官能，
而只是其中一個部分而已。

你可曾想過：我們是如何浪費生命、消耗能量的？我們又是如何成為「二手人類」，只會吸取他人智慧的？不論是生理上還是心理上的乏味、煩惱、孤獨、痛苦，都已完全佔據了我們的生活。就在當下，我們的生命已經毫無意義，因為我們只是單純為了活著而活著。除此之外，我們的整個生命以及內在的心靈，已然支離破碎，不再完整。

我們需要什麼？我們已經得到了什麼？對於大多數人來說，生命充滿了艱辛、困苦和衝突。

在當前這個社會，物質財富已經成為衡量一個人成功與否的標準。我們奔波在追求權力、地位和聲譽的路上，過著平庸、狹隘、淺薄和空虛的生活，並深受各種觀念、判斷和信仰的影響與左右。所有這一切，都是在浪費和揮霍生命。

我們不曾有過幸福，只不過是在追求享樂的過程中產生片刻的愉悅和滿足。但當你深入反省自我時，是否發現內心深處其實除了過去攝取的書本知識和對所處社會的回饋之外一無所有？而那一切，也不過是思想的創造。但思想並不能代表人的所有身體官能，而只是其中的一個部分而已。

在意識到生命的空虛——毋寧說是生命的淺薄和痛苦之後，我們開始追求享樂（不論宗教意義上的喜悅還是所謂世俗的快樂），開始追逐物質財富、更高級的享受和更多的快樂，購買更多的物品，維持消費型社會的運轉，直到最終走向墳墓。這就是我們的生命，既談不上神聖，亦無關乎宗教。

但生命本應是極其嚴肅的事，只有那些真正嚴肅對待生命的人，他們的生活才有意義。反之，如果一味遵從宗教導師、牧師、智者或哲學家的訓導，人就會失去自我，生活就會失去意義。

於是，有人會問：思想在我們的生命中處於何種位置？人類所有的文明、文化，都是以思想為基礎。宗教是思想的產物，行為、操行、商業世界、人際關係、軍備積累、陸軍、海軍、空軍，所有這一切都是基於思想之上的。不管思想是否合理、是否合乎邏輯、是否健全，我們的行動都是以思想為基礎的。然而，思想還只是想法，是一種理想，由此看來，我們每個人都是極端的唯心主義者，這真是十分不幸。

實際上，理想並不等於「實相」，而只是思想創造出來、用以應對「實相」的方法。理想和「實相」之間實則存在差異與衝突。

我希望你並不僅僅去傾聽，而是要切實地觀察內心的整個運作過程，從而與之建立交流的關係。也就是說如實觀照，而不加諸任何判斷。

我們一定要探究何為思想，何為思考。在亞洲人看來，思想是最不同尋常的事物之一，猶如鳳毛麟角。他們認為思想是一種量度，若想要尋求不可測量的，也就是超越時間與量度的事物，人就必須要挑戰思想。而恰恰與之相反，整個西方文明社會與文化都是建立在思想之上。

正如我所說，生命是非常嚴肅的事，需要用心探究。我希望你已經做好了求知的準備，可以免於量度的限制，去瞭解那無邊的空寂──這種空寂無法衡量，也非思想所能創造。

此前說過，西方文明與文化是建立在思想之上、可以量度的。由此，整個科技的世界得以形成並發展。在這個世界裡，宗教成了一種值得信仰、接納、宣傳乃至可以救世的東西。

在東方，思想已經超越了其原有的含義；而在西方，人們則接受思想這一量度的延伸拓展，基於科技成就的生活方式讓他們獲得了越來越多的享受，而擁有財產（其中包括文學和詩歌）也給他們帶來了極大的快樂。

嚴肅看待生命的人必定會問及思想在生命中的地位究竟如何。思想積聚了過多來自內在與外界的資訊，其中有的資訊是健全、合乎邏輯而理性的，有的卻是導向墮落的生活，唯物質、財產、金錢和快樂至上。這樣的思想究竟有何作用？它處於怎樣的地位，與行動之間的關係又是如何？因為生命即是行動力，關係則是行動力的具體運作。那麼在我們的生命中，有沒有一種行為，可以不受時間、思想和量度制約？

　　生活即是行動。我們所做的一切都是行動，而如果這些行動自始至終（從過去到現在到將來）都受到限制，那麼它永遠都不會得到解脫，永遠都不會完整。這樣的行動就是墮落的。

　　那麼，什麼是行動？行動與思想之間又有何關係？思想是記憶的反應，而記憶正是由存儲在大腦裡的知識和經驗所構成的。沒必要翻閱神經學或科學類書籍，只要你有濃厚的興趣，觀察自己的思想就足以瞭解到相關情形了。沒有記憶，你就不能行動，就無法記住說過的話。這樣一來，你就會陷入健忘狀態，以致生活混亂不堪。

　　思想可依據自身的條件對外界產生行動反應。如果你是一名基督教徒、佛教徒、共產主義者或資本主義者，你的心就會受限於此，而你的行動也會以此為依據。以你對自己所處的特定文化或社會的記憶、經驗和知識為依據。這是非常明顯的，不是嗎？因此，行動中的思想是破碎的、不完整的，並會導致衝突。

　　我們必須要理解這一點，因為我們正試圖尋找一種完全沒有衝突、沒有痛苦，完整、純粹、和諧而健全的生活方式。而思想可能是導致生活不完整乃至墮落的因素之一。因此，我們必須瞭解思想的作用所在，以及思想在人類關係中所處的位置。

　　眾所周知，在科技領域，思想的作用是至關重要的。在知識領域，思想的作用合理、健全、客觀、有效。但當思想希望通過科技確立地位時，這種有效性、健全性和客觀性就會大打折扣。顯而易見，儘管依然會作出合乎邏輯、健全而理性的思考，但由於受環境影響至深，你還是會尋求地位的確立。這樣一來，衝突將不可避免地持續下去，而生活亦因此墮落。墮落並不僅僅是指攫取他人錢財或者做不道德的事情；墮落的深層原因是思想將行動分裂為以下幾個片段——智慧行動、情緒行動、身體行動或意識形態行動。

那麼，在人類關係中，有沒有一種行動是以完整而非片段的形式呈現，可以不受思想、量度或過去所控制？當你說話時，當你對他人表示不敬或表示歡迎時，這些都是行動。在某種意義上，行動可以說是無處不在，它可能是依據某個規則，根據某個觀念，基於某種想法或某個理想，甚至是出於某種空想或信仰而為之的。總而言之，行動是基於某種過去的思維模式，或者基於某種有關未來的抽象觀念。

生命中最重要的基礎是關係。行為、美德、操行和人際交往皆源於關係。思想總是要求人們依照既有結論來行事，而結論通常源於過去的知識。那麼，思想在人類關係中處於何種位置？抑或根本就毫無地位？如果人類關係中有思想的一席之地，那思想就會制約並掌控關係，使之產生分裂與衝突。

我們的生命基於兩個原則：快樂和恐懼。你可以觀察自我，由此發現快樂已經在生命中變得極為重要，並且有各種形式：性愛的快樂，獲得智慧的快樂，佔有財物的快樂，取得權力或名譽的快樂，自我重視的快樂，自我論斷的快樂，以及通過暴力獲取的某種快樂，等等。而在關係中，快樂的表現爲依戀——你在心理上依戀於關係中的另一方，並因此感到快樂。只要存在這種依戀，那麼必有對失去的恐懼，而對失去的恐懼又進一步強化了這種依戀心理。這在追求性愛的快樂上表現得尤爲明顯。最不可思議的是，這種快樂已經成爲生命中最重要的事。這就是依戀式的快樂——在心理上依賴於他人，因爲人一向害怕孤獨，害怕失去愛或是不被人愛。因此，人總是追求快樂，逃避恐懼。而思想則令你懷念昨日的快樂，並希望今天也能得到昨日那樣的快樂。如果快樂不再持續，你就會變得暴躁、焦慮、恐懼。對於上述種種，你可以從自己身上觀察到。

現在讓我們看看恐懼這個問題。伴隨著恐懼的生活是黑暗、醜陋的。我們大多數人都會產生恐懼情緒，只是恐懼的物件不盡相同。那我們的心能否完全免於恐懼呢？沒有人希望生活中沒有快樂，而所有的人都希望自己的生活遠離恐懼；你看不到以上兩者之間的並列關係，它們就像是同一枚硬幣的兩面，都是由思想維持著。

對思想的理解之所以如此重要，原因就在於此。因爲我們心中有著深深的不安全感，懷有各種各樣的恐懼：對死亡的恐懼，對生活、黑暗、鄰里、自我、失業的恐懼，還有隱藏在內心深處不爲人知的其他恐懼，等等。因此，我們努力尋求安全感。然而，我們的心究竟有無可能完全免於恐懼，可以眞正去享受生活而非追求短暫的快樂？實際上，只要存在恐懼感，我們就不可能享受生活。

那麼，分析能夠消除恐懼嗎？還是說，分析致使心靈無法避免恐懼？讓我們探尋一下這其中隱含的關係。

人們已經習慣了分析——它相當於一種需要智慧的娛樂活動。在分析中，無論分析者是專業人士還是你自己，都存在分析者與被分析者之分，這兩者之間必然會產生分裂與衝突。此外，分析需要時間，你往往需要數天乃至數年的時間來分析，行動則因此而延遲。比如說，你可以無限期地分析暴力問題，探究其根源，並聽取不同專家的解釋，查閱有關資料，並對這些根源加以分析。所有的這一切都需要時間，而在此期間，暴力問題並未解決。分析意味著分裂，意味著行動的延遲——所以分析只會增加而不會減少衝突。此外，分析還意味著要耗費很多時間。

明瞭上述道理的人是不會糾纏於分析之中的，因而也就有能力直接應對內心的暴躁——此即當下的實相。如果你能夠全面觀察內在的暴躁（這種暴躁源自於你的恐懼、不安全感、孤獨、依戀與追求快樂），不做分析，那麼就可以將用來做分析的精力轉用於解決實際問題上。

這個社會賦予了我們根深蒂固、與過去息息相關的恐懼感，它們能否一一呈現出來，以使我們可以完全從中解脫，免受折磨？我們能否觀察到恐懼的整體，還是說只能觀察到它的散枝末節？我們能否全然專注地去觀察、領會、瞭解恐懼（不管它是隱藏在我們的內心深處還是顯現於外）——以避免昨日的痛苦仍會在今日或明日重現？恐懼的形態多種多樣，包括對失業的恐懼、對外界或內在缺少安全感的恐懼、對死亡的終極恐懼等等，不一而足。我們是否應該剪掉恐懼的散枝末葉，將其作為一個整體來瞭解？

我們已經習慣於應對片段化的恐懼，例如害怕失去工作、失去妻子或丈夫，然而這些都不是恐懼的整體。想觀察恐懼的整體，必須在產生恐懼時，傾注全部的注意力去觀察。

作為觀察者，當我們看著自己的憤怒、妒忌、羨慕、恐懼甚至快樂時，總希望能夠擺脫它們。通常，觀察者也是目擊者、思考者，觀察恐懼就好像從外向內觀察一樣。觀察者是處於過去的，他先是識別出對所謂恐懼的反應，然後才將其命名為「恐懼」。由於觀察者總是從過去觀察現在，所以和被觀察者之間就產生了分裂。那麼，如果沒有對過去的反應，沒有觀察者，你還能否觀察到恐懼？

比如說，我過去遇見過你，你侮辱或恭維過我，做過很多抵制或是支持我的事。所有這一切都已是過去的累積記憶。過去既是觀察者，也是思考者，當對方看你時，是以過去而非現在的眼光看你的。所以，觀察者永遠都不會對你做出正確的觀察，因為他看待你的眼光已經變質，已經遲鈍。那麼，如果沒有了過去的干擾，你還能否觀察到恐懼？這意味著不去定義「恐懼」之意，不使用「恐懼」一詞，而只是純粹地觀察。

事實是，只有在沒有觀察者，即在沒有過去的情況下，你才有可能集中全部的注意力去進行真正的觀察，從而將恐懼從意識中完全消除。

恐懼既有來自外部的，也有生髮於內在的。譬如我害怕兒子在戰爭中死去。戰爭即是外部的恐懼來源——在科技的推動下，威力無比的戰爭武器層出不窮。而在內心深處，我深愛著我的兒子，教育他遵從社會的生存法則，也就是殺戮。當人們關注的是佔有財富、消費至上，而非世界和人類的整體發展時，社會就是墮落而不正常的。

我們雖然擁有豐富的知識和經驗，可以在醫學領域、科學技術領域取得非凡的成就，但卻沒有任何憐憫心。憐憫心意味著對所有人類、動物和大自然的熱愛。當心懷恐懼，而又不停地追求快樂時，又怎麼會有憐憫心呢？人們既希望得到快樂，又希望控制恐懼、將之隱藏，同時還想要擁有憐憫心，但往往事不遂願。因為只有在恐懼完全消失的時候，人才會有憐憫心。之所以說極有必要瞭解存於我們關係中的恐懼，原因就在於此。對於任何一種反應，當你只是觀察它而不加諸定義時，恐懼才會徹底根除。將反應命名為「恐懼」，實際上是對過去的一種投射。因此，思想還會繼續存在，還會繼續追求快樂，同時賦予恐懼以力量，讓人們害怕來日可能發生的事情，害怕失去工作，害怕時間，害怕死亡。

因此，思想是造成恐懼的原因。生活在思想中，我們的日常活動是建立在思想之上的。思想在人類關係中處於何種位置？你曾經侮辱或恭維過我，這在我腦海中留下了記憶，留下了痕跡，而當我再看你的時候自然就會帶著這種記憶。因此，我對你的看法必然帶有過去的烙印。之所以說很有必要瞭解思想在關係中所處的位置，原因就在於此。如果思想在關係中擁有一席之地，那麼關係就會成為日常生活的例行常規，就會變得呆板、機械，充滿毫無意義的快樂和恐懼。

於是就有人問：什麼是愛？愛是思想的產物嗎？不幸的是，愛已經成為思想製造的產物——我們「愛」上帝，「愛」人類，同時又幹著破壞大自然的行徑。

我們必須深入探究這一問題，明白到底什麼是愛，因為沒有愛、沒有憐憫的話，我們只會遭受苦難。而想要找到愛，想要擁有強大的憐憫心，則必須瞭解苦難，因為熱愛是苦難造就的結果。

「熱愛」一詞的基本義就是悲傷和苦難，而大多數人都想要逃脫苦難。我並不是說必須接受生理或心理上的苦難。那是愚蠢的。但思想是苦難的運動嗎？抑或，苦難是完全不同於思想的東西？

瞭解思考的整個運轉機制很重要，這並不僅僅是言詞上的理解，而是我們自身要切實觀察何為思考，以理解思考與日常生活之間的關係。

第三章 | 死亡的意義

死亡意味著我們已知的所有事物的終結。
所依戀的一切都將煙消雲散，
積累的所有財富亦無法帶走。

人的一生，多碌碌無為。雖精力旺盛，卻未用於正途，時間多花在辦公室裡，或用於整理花園。這種人可能是一名律師，也可能是一個遁世者。綜而觀之，人的一生似乎毫無意義，沒有任何重要性可言。而當他到了五十歲、八十歲或九十歲回望人生時，他就會問自己這一生都做過什麼。

生命具有最為非凡的意義，有至美，有大苦，有深憂。然而，當這一切都結束的時候，我們可曾想過自己這一生都做過些什麼？我們的生命裡，多半充斥著金錢、性、生存的持續衝突、倦怠、辛勞、不幸、挫折以及偶有的快樂；又或者，你一輩子都在全身心地愛著一個人，而完全沒有自我。

世上似無公平可言。哲學家已經對公平做了諸多論述。人人希望得到公平。但生命中真有公平存在嗎？一個人生性機敏、社會地位高、頭腦聰慧、相貌英俊、擁有任何他想要的東西，而另一個人卻一文不名；一個人受過良好的教育、擁有豐富的知識、可以做任何想做的事，另一個人卻是身心俱殘；一個人能說善寫，堪爲模範，另一個人卻與之相反；一個人光明正大，而另一個人詭計多端；一個人聰明、懂事、敏感、細膩、喜歡美麗日落與朗月清輝，能夠看到世間萬物，另一個人卻目不能視；一個人是理性、健全、健康的，而另一個人不是。

所以你看，這世上眞有公平嗎？人類可曾得到過公平？環顧周遭，生命對大多數人來說是如此的空虛，又是如此的毫無意義。法律面前人人平等，但有錢人比沒錢人更容易受到法律的保護，因爲他們可以聘請優秀的律師爲其辯護。有的人出身高貴，而有的人出身貧賤。這個問題已經涉及哲學層面，涉及對眞理與生命的熱愛。或許，眞理就存在於生命中，而不是在書本上和思想中——它與生命密不可分。所謂眞理，可能就是我們住在哪里，又以何種方式生活。

觀察世間諸事，顯然其中並不存在公平。那麼，公平又在哪里呢？似乎只有在具備憐憫心的時候才存在公平。然而憐憫心既不源於任何宗教，也並非來自於任何教派。迷信和神明不會讓你成爲一個富有憐憫心的人。要想擁有憐憫心，你必須要擺脫所有的束縛，擁有全然的自由。但這樣的自由可能存在嗎？

人類的大腦已經過了數百萬年的進化，這是事實。而我們接受的知識越多，對天地萬物的瞭解越多，內心也就越發困惑。哪里有憐憫，哪里就有智慧，而哪里有智慧，哪里就有公平的願景。我們創造了因果報應和輪回轉世的概念，並認爲可以通過這些構想出未來的概念或理論體系,來解決公平的問題。但實際上,只有當心靈完全澄淨,並懷有憐憫時,公平才會存在。

我們的大腦是一種非常複雜的器械。無論你我,都擁有一顆人類的大腦,它的進化時間並不僅限於從我們出生直到現在,而是已經歷了極其漫長的歲月,並深深影響著我們的意識。這裡說的並不是個人的意識,而是指全人類的智性基石。當你觀察這種意識中的信仰、信條、觀念、恐懼、快樂、痛苦、孤獨、沮喪和絕望時,會發現它並不是自己獨有的個人意識。我們一直認為自己是獨立的個體,但實際上,並不存在「你的大腦」或「我的大腦」之分別,我們並非彼此分離。

我們深受教育體制和宗教觀念的影響,總認為自己是獨立的個人,擁有獨立的靈魂。但實際上,我們根本不是獨立的個體,而是數千年來人類經驗、努力和抗爭的結果。因此,我們深受限制,從未擁有過自由。

事實是,只要仍然依照某種觀念、結論而生活,或是生活在特定的理念或理想中,那我們的大腦就不會獲得自由,因而也就不可能擁有憐憫。而這種自由是指從印度教徒、基督教徒、伊斯蘭教徒或佛教徒的身份中解放出來,免於被特殊化的自由(雖然許多人並不拒絕特殊化),免于成為金錢的奴隸。

只要大腦依然像現在一樣被限制,人類就不會有自由。正如部分哲學家和生物學家所說的,知識的提升空間已經達到極限。在駕駛、經商、旅行以及科研等方面，知識是必要的。但一個人記憶中所積累的關於自我的心理學知識——那其實是外界壓力和內在需求的產物——卻毫無存在的必要。

生命總是破碎、片段化和分裂的。它們從未完整過，我們也從未對它做過完整的觀察，而總是從某個特定的角度去看待。由於我們自身本就是分裂的，所以總是被我們以分別心看待的生命本身也是矛盾重重、衝突不斷。

我們從未把生命看成是完整一體、不可分裂的——這裡的「完整」既有健康、健全之意，又可理解爲神聖，是一個非常重要的詞。之所以重要，並不是因爲它可以將不同的片段融入人類的意識中。我們一直試圖調和不同的矛盾。那麼，我們有沒有可能將生命視爲整體，將苦難、快樂、痛苦、焦慮、孤獨、上班、擁有住房、性、擁有子女等諸多非獨立的活動視爲包羅萬象的完整運動呢？這有可能嗎？抑或，我們必須永遠生活在分裂的片段式衝突中？

我們有沒有可能觀察這些片段並對它們進行確認——只是觀察，不去糾正、不過度解讀、不回避、不壓制？問題並不在於要做什麼，因爲不管你做什麼，你的行動都是源自於片段式的生活，這樣一來，也就會製造出更多的片段和分裂。相反的，如果你能夠觀察生命的整個運動，將其視爲一個整體，那麼不僅衝突的破壞力會消失，而且還會爲你帶來一種全新的生活方式。

我想知道的是，人們是否發現自己的生活已經支離破碎？而當他們發現了，會否想要知道如何再將這些碎片拼湊為整體？那麼誰才是那個獨立存在並生活的實體？是「我」嗎？又是誰來將那些碎片拼湊起來？所謂的實體是否也只是碎片？思想本身即是片段化的，因為知識沒有窮盡，它是記憶的累積，而思想是記憶的反應，因而思想也是受限的。思想永遠無法幫助人去全面地觀察生命。

那麼，人能否將片段式的生活作為一個整體來觀察？這個人可以是專家、教師或一家之主，也可能是遁世之人。如果沒有了觀察者，人能否從某個片斷中觀察到生命的整體運動？觀察者即是過去，即是累積的記憶，也就代表了時間的量度。過去正在看著這個片段，而其本身又是更早之前的記憶片段的產物。

那麼，如果沒有時間，沒有思想，沒有對過去的記憶，也沒有語言，我們是否還可以觀察？因為語言並非事物，同樣是源自於過去的。人們常通過字詞的分拆與釋義來認知，而那無非是語言的一種運動。我們從未有過直接感知——那種感知即是可以改變腦細胞本身的洞見。不過，雖然時間和思考機能導致我們的大腦受限，並長期處於固定思維之中，但無論對於任何問題，只要全然專注地去觀察，就會改變細胞結構，形成直接感知。

我們已經創造出了關於何時可以如願與達到成就的「心理時間」概念。我們就是這種源於思想的內在時間的主宰者，而這也正是我們必須要瞭解時間本質的原因。為什麼人類會創造出所謂的心理時間或內在時間——譬如說何時能過上幸福生活，何時能免遭暴力，何時能獲得快樂，又可以在何時擁有崇高心境，進入冥想之境？但事實是，只要是在時間的涵蓋範圍之內，人的任何活動都會有矛盾與衝突。所謂心理時間即意味著衝突。

所謂過去、現在和未來，都不過是心理學概念上的時間。如果人能夠意識到這條真理，那將是個偉大的發現。我們總認為生與死之間還有一段遙遠的時間距離，認為生活就是生活，死亡則是要努力避免和延遲的事，這其實是將生命的另一個片段放在了遙遠的未來。要想全面觀察整個生命的運動，人就不該將生與死區隔看待。但問題是，人只在意生存問題，而不關心死亡，甚至不願談及。因此，人不僅是從生理上把生命片段化，而且還把自己的生活和死亡分離了開來。

那麼，什麼是死亡？難道它不是生命的一部分？也許人人都害怕死亡，都希望能夠延長生命、避免死亡，但死亡終究會到來。

什麼是生活？它屬於我們的意識範疇嗎？實際上，是生活的內容構成了我們的種種意識，生活的內容與意識並無二致。人所信仰的、崇拜的，以及相關的神明、儀式；人的貪婪、野心、好勝心；人內心深處的孤獨、依戀、苦難……所有這一切都構成了意識。但它們並非某一個人自己的意識，而是全體人類所共有的意識。個人即是世界，世界即是個人。人即是由意識及其內容構成。

人類正是基於上述的意識內容而存活。因此，無論從心理學上還是內在層面來講，人都不是獨立存在的。從外表看，人或許彼此有別，有黃色、棕色或黑色人種之分，又有個子高矮、男性女性的差異，但從深層次的內在來看，我們卻是相似的，或許稍有不同，但其實就像是串在同一根線上的珠子。

我們必須要理解何為生活，然後才能夠回答何為死亡。死亡之前的事情畢竟要比死亡之後發生的事更重要。那麼，生活是與他人毫無關係的辛勞和衝突嗎？或者，深層的、內在的孤獨感就是我們所說的生活？為了逃避這樣的生活，你會前往教堂、寺廟，去做毫無意義的祈禱與膜拜；如果有錢，你就會鋪張揚厲。但其實你做的所有這一切都是為了逃避自己的意識與心境，而這就是所謂的生活。

死亡意味著我們已知的所有事物的終結。依戀的一切都將煙消雲散，積累的所有財富亦無法帶走──你會因此感到害怕，恐懼已成為你生命的一部分。然而，不論你是誰，多麼富有或貧窮，即便位居要職、擁有無上權力，都終有一死。

但死去的是什麼？是「我」，是這一生的積累，包括所有的痛苦、孤獨、絕望、淚水、歡笑和苦難。所有這一切加總起來，構成了「我」。你或許會辯解，說在內心深處還有一種更崇高的心靈，包括自我與靈魂，皆是永恆之物，但這些其實都源於思想。而思想並非神聖不可侵犯的東西。

人所依戀的只是一個「我」，而「我」終會死亡──我們的生命便是如此。生命屬於已知，死亡屬於未知。而我們既害怕已知的東西，又恐懼未知的事物。

死亡是對過去、現在和將來，也就是「我」的完全否定。而正是出於對死亡的恐懼，你認為人類還會以其他的生命形態存在，並且相信輪迴轉世之說。這其實是那些不明白何為生存的人一廂情願的想法而已。他們認為生活充滿了無盡的痛苦、衝突和苦難，而歡笑與快樂只是曇花一現。他們會說，「我們還會有來生，我在死後，還會遇到我的妻子或丈夫、我的兒子、我的神。」人們還不明白自己是什麼，又依戀什麼。人必須深入而認真地去探究這種依戀。人必須明白，死亡會褫奪所有，它不允許我們帶走任何東西。

　　死亡是生命的一部分。人類的大腦能否從對死亡的恐懼中解脫？作為心理時間的主宰者，人能否與死亡同行而不是想要逃避、延遲或離棄它，並能理解終結的意義——也就是理解否定的意義，去否定自己的依戀與信仰？否定和終結將會帶來全新的事物。那麼，人能否在活著的時候完全否定依戀？此即與死亡同行。

　　死亡在生命中具有非凡的意義。我們說的不是自殺或安樂死，而是在說對他人的依戀、自尊心、對抗心理乃至憎惡感的終結。如果你能將生命作為一個整體來觀察，就會發現死亡、生存、煩惱、絕望、孤獨和苦難都處於同一個運動的整體中，你就不會再害怕死亡。而死亡即意味著生命沒有延續，若能認知到這一點，那麼即便身體將要毀壞，你也不會再對無法延續感到恐懼。

　　當你全面、系統地理解了死亡的全部意義，也就擺脫了意識的束縛。在你的生命歷程中，生與死始終一體、相伴相隨，死亡其實

一直都在你的身邊。與死亡同行，這是最為非凡的體驗。沒有過
去、現在，也沒有將來，只有終結。

第四章 ┃ 理解愛

愛不是感覺，不是快樂、
欲望和滿足，也不是嫉妒、憎恨。
有愛的人，就有同情心，
而且得體、大方，
但這些特質都不等於愛。

各種思想之間是彼此關聯的。它們構成了一系列被我們稱爲思考的運動。沒有一種思想可以單獨存在，而不與其他思想毫無關聯。此外，顯而易見的是，思考就是我們的生命。

當你追逐一種思想，別的思想也會隨之而來。例如我在擦鞋的時候，視線卻飄向窗外，去欣賞秀美山巒，便停下了手上的工作，隨後又必須要回過神來繼續擦鞋。我希望能夠集中注意力，但思想卻飄到了另一個方向，於是接下來我試圖收回思緒，繼續專注於手頭的事情。

自孩提時代起直至死亡，我們會時常遇到這樣的情形。而你越是思考，心中的想法就會越來越多：「我必須往正確的方向思考，不應該去想這些事情。」「是否存在正確的思考、錯誤的思考和有目的的思考？」「生命的目的是什麼？」諸如此類的念頭不一而足，可見思考的整個過程是沒有終點的。

思想做過很多非凡之事。在科技領域，它的貢獻令人震撼甚至恐懼。它創造了所有折磨人的宗教儀式，將我們從一個地方驅逐到另一個地方。此外，不論是西方還是東方的思想，本質都是思考，而不會有東方式思考和西方式思考之區別。

那麼，思想有無盡頭？這並不是在問你的思考，也不是問我的思考，而是問我們所有人的思考會否朝著同一個方向運動，最終達致某個終點？也就是說，時間會不會有盡頭？

思考是知識的產物，是記憶的產物。人是需要付出時間來獲得知識的。即便是性能非凡的電腦，也需要片刻的時間才能夠給出答案。因此，當我們問思想有沒有盡頭時，也就是在問時間有沒有終點。如果深究下去，你會發現這是一個相當有趣的問題。

時間對我們意味著什麼？這裡所說的時間並不僅限於心理層面，還包括外在感知的層面，比如說日落、日出，學習一門語言花費的時間，等等。我們從一個地方去到另一個地方，從這裡走到那裡，即便是搭乘速度最快的火車或飛機，也都需要時間。

然而，在「現實」和「可能成為現實」、「我是什麼」和「我將是什麼」之間，必然存在距離，不管這距離是短如剎那還是長達幾個世紀，它都只能用時間來丈量。因此，時間意味著進化。就好像你在地裡播下的種子需要一整個季節的時間才能夠成長、成熟，甚至需要一千年光陰才能長成參天大樹。任何事物的成長或轉變都需要時間，無一例外。因此，時間和思想並非兩個獨立的運動，而是同一種運動。

我們並不是要探究時間的永恆與否，只是在問思想和時間究竟有無盡頭——這是個非常嚴肅的、人類自誕生以來便面臨的問題之一。那麼，你將如何尋找答案？通過分析？通過所謂的直覺？

作為一個被過度使用的詞，「直覺」或許是最危險的。它可能代表了我們內心深處的欲望與動機，亦反映出我們自身的傾向、特質、特定知識的積累情況。而在這裡，我想問的是，如果你對所有這一切都不予考慮，那麼對你而言時間有無終點？你必須自己去尋找答案，而不是去問別人，因為別人說什麼於你而言都沒有意義。

我們必須從更深的層次來探討時間的本質，就如同探究思考的本質一樣。所有的一切都會走向盡頭嗎？時間是漸進的過程嗎？如果是，那麼這種漸進性就是時間的本質，而時間也就不可能有終點。無論是下個週末還是明天，或是幾分鐘之後、下一秒鐘，都不可能稱之為某個時段的結束。

如果你能真正明白這一點，深刻理解了思想與時間的本質、秩序和生活的藝術，不再將時間視為終會結束的運動，而平和地與之共處，那麼你就可以一窺時間的本質。而且，有關時間的洞見與記憶無關，與其他任何事物都無關。你只管去尋找吧！

有些人可能會很輕鬆地說，是的，時間存在終點。這種說法非常幼稚。除非真正去調查、去體驗、去發現和深究，否則我們不會產生那種奇異的永恆之感。

我們狹隘的大腦如何才能掌握那些廣闊無邊的事物？這絕不可

能，因爲大腦自身的局限性根深蒂固。我們應當清楚以下事實（不是想法而是事實），即大腦是受知識、專業、特定學科以及我們所屬的團體和民族特性限制的。從本質上講，無非是人類對自我利益的欲求（它就隱藏在長袍、王冠、儀式之類的事物背後）導致了大腦的這種局限性。這是非常明顯的。當我關注自己的幸福、成就與能否成功時，這種自我利益的欲求就會限制大腦的特性與活力。

數百萬年來，人類的大腦一直在時間、死亡和思考中進化，這就意味著一系列的時間進程。在這樣的進程中，大腦總是會首先尋求自身的安全，將自己置於「安全地帶」，因而就會說出「我認爲」、「我不認爲」、「我同意」、「我不同意」、「這是我的看法」、「這是我的判斷」之類的話。不論說話者是宗教人士、知名政客還是名利場中人或者知識淵博的教授，抑或是大談良善與和平的教派領袖，這麼說都是出於保護自我利益的考量。

如今，我們的大腦已經變小——這並不是說它的形狀或尺寸變小，而是說它的能力已經大爲減弱。在科技領域，大腦創造出了巨大的成就，但就內在而言，大腦同樣具有的無限能力已經被自我利益限制了。自我利益的藏身之處很難尋得，它或許藏在某種幻想之中，或是隱於神經質、虛僞的個性乃至宗族姓氏之中。去掀開每一塊石頭，檢查每一片草葉，找到它吧。

不過，你若是花費時間去尋找，這又會成爲一種束縛；你也可以只是去觀察，於當下去瞭解。當你完全洞察之後，那洞見就會涵蓋你的整個內在。

受限的大腦如何才能領悟無遠弗屆的美、愛和眞理？憐憫和智慧又在哪里？我們每一個人都能與之相遇嗎？你邀請憐憫了嗎？你邀請智慧了嗎？你邀請美、愛和眞理了嗎？你有沒有試圖理解它？我問的是你。你有沒有試圖去理解智慧與憐憫，以及無限的美感、愛的芬芳和無處可循的眞理？這些就是你希望尋找並理解的嗎？受限的大腦能否領悟它們？

無論你如何努力，都不可能掌握並領悟它們──即便去冥想、齋戒、苦行、清修，只擁有一件衣服。富人與窮人都無法領悟最終的眞理，那些發誓終生獨身、保持緘默或苦行度日的人同樣不會獲得眞理。他們尋找眞理的行爲是由思想反復權衡而決定的，是有意而爲。由於大腦受限，所以你將要做的任何事情都是受限的；蓮花趺坐、發呆、冥想、倒立或單腿站立──不管你做什麼，都受到了限制，憐憫並不會因此出現。

因此，你必須理解什麼是愛。愛不是感覺，不是快樂、欲望和滿足，也不是嫉妒、憎恨。有愛的人，就有憐憫心，而且得體、大方，但這些特質都不等於愛。要想理解和領悟此點，你還需要極佳的美感和審美意識。這裡所說的美並非男女的相貌之美，並非電影明星的氣質之美。美不在於高山上、溪穀中，也不在於天空或是河流裡。美，只存在於有愛的地方。美和愛的本質，都是憐憫。

然而憐憫不會待在你觸手可及的地方。美、愛、眞理，是智慧的最高表現形式。而有智慧的地方，就有行動，就有明性，就有莫大的尊嚴。這是常人無法想像之事，因而也是無法用語言來表達的。雖然它可以被描述，而哲學家也已經進行了描述，但他們所描述的其實並不是愛。

要想理解這種感覺，就不能以「我」、「自我」為中心來行動或尋求轉變。你必須保持極大的靜默。靜意味著萬事皆空，這巨大的空無中蘊藏著無窮的能量——並非自我利益的能量，而是不受限制的能量。

死亡是最不尋常的事情，是對生命延續性的終結。在生命延續的期間，我們總是希望確保安全，因為大腦只有在完全安全的狀態下才能保持最佳工作狀態——這種安全包括不受恐怖威脅、擁有信仰與求知的自由，等等。但所有的一切都會因死亡的到來而結束。我或許期望擁有來生，但死亡卻結束了生命的長期延續。我已經把自己視為這種延續性本身。死亡卻會說：「對不起，老夥計，這一切要結束了。」其實你沒有必要害怕死亡，只需正視它，與終結者同在。死亡所結束的，只是你過去的生活、記憶與經歷。

時間給了我們希望，思想給了我們慰藉，並向我們保證了生命是可以延續的。於是我們說：「好吧，在來生……」只要不放棄這種荒唐、愚蠢的幻想，也許真的有來生——這就是時間和思想給予我們的關於延續性的保證，我們依戀於此，因而也就會產生恐懼。而恐懼將摧毀愛。但在實質上，愛、憐憫和死亡是密不可分的。

我們能夠與死亡同行嗎？思想和時間有終點嗎？所有這些問題都是彼此關聯的。不要把時間、思想和死亡分離開來。它們是同一事物。

第五章 ｜ 傾聽、觀察與學習

傾聽，必不可預設方向。
觀察，必不可有歪曲。
而學習，必有觀察與注視的自由。
如果能夠擁有這三種日常生活的藝術，
就能過上真正安寧、和諧的生活。

每個人都應仔細瞭解傾聽、觀察和學習的藝術。「藝術」一詞是用在藝術家身上的，比如說畫家、詩人、雕塑家，等等。「藝術」這個詞的本義是指讓萬物（如我們的思想、情感以及憂慮等等）各就其位、適得其所，從而達至均衡、和諧。

　　我們很少聽得進別人的話。我們有自己的結論、經驗，有自己的問題和判斷──它們充斥了我們的內在，以致再也沒有任何傾聽的空間。

　　然而，只有拋開原有的觀點、知識、問題和結論，才有可能去傾聽，而且在傾聽時也不會做出多餘的解讀、判斷和評價。

　　實際上，傾聽的藝術就在於全神貫注、充滿感情地去聽。如果你能夠掌握這一點，就能夠與他人無礙地交流，一起思考，一起分享，一起分擔。生活在這樣一個世界裡，周圍充滿了許多醜陋、兇殘、狂暴且毫無存在意義的事物，交流對我們來說顯然非常重要。

　　傾聽的藝術可以幫助你快速學習、發現真相。我們所聽到的每一個詞之間的細微差別都具有重要意義，傾聽之中存有無限自由，可以讓你即刻領悟其中的意涵，形成洞見。除了傾聽之外，還有觀察的藝術，即觀察事物的眞實面目，而不是帶著自己的意願去觀察；同時不應帶有任何幻想或預設任何判斷和看法，要看到眞正的實相，而不要妄下結論。

此外，還有學習的藝術。學習的藝術並不在於記憶。記憶會讓人變得非常呆板，我們的大腦早已經被機械化了。學習的藝術意味著自由地觀察，不帶偏見地傾聽，沒有爭論，沒有任何情緒上的或不切實際的反應。

如果我們能夠擁有這三種日常生活的藝術，將諸事物各歸原位，那麼就能眞正過上安寧、和諧的生活。因此，請現在就開始學習傾聽的藝術。

請認眞去聽。思想是時間，是量度，是時間中的一種運動，並創造了恐懼。如果你不去對這一論述下定論，而是用心傾聽，全神貫注地聽，那恐懼在你心中將毫無立足之地。這就是傾聽的藝術創造的奇跡。

因此，去傾聽吧，不必想著該怎麼做。傾聽者應是敏感、機靈、警覺的。如果你能夠掌握傾聽的技巧，自然就可以正確對待心中的諸種思想，從而與他人和善相處，而不會產生衝突。

我們的意識即是日常生活的反映。意識中包含有權力的欲望，有我們自孩提時代起就遭受的諸多傷害，也有恐懼、快樂、所謂的愛（但實際上並不是愛），還有無數的信仰——信仰神或無神、信仰社會主義或資本主義。信仰意味著人的生活是建立在虛構之上、毫無實質內容的。

意識並非沒有秩序，它的秩序源於傾聽、觀察和學習。傾聽，必不可預設方向。觀察，必不可有歪曲。而學習，並非記憶，而是必有觀察與注視的自由。

第六章 ｜ 冥想的基礎

我們經常會產生幻想，
認為自己已經進入了冥想狀態，
但如果日常生活中沒有秩序，
那麼不管是在做什麼，
都不可能是冥想。
因此，
我們必須奠定冥想的基礎，
也就是秩序。

我經常想，為什麼大家會聚到一起，半是認真半是好奇地去聽別人演講，卻又不是真的想要改變自己的生活。我們已經變得如此平庸，毫無天分，沒有任何天才的品質。我所說的「天才」，並非指具有某種特定的才能或天賦，而是指能夠完全理解生命的本質是一個巨大、複雜、相互對立的不幸存在。

人們雖然會去傾聽他人的演講，但卻一知半解，從未認真想過要在內心深處進行一場心理革命。我經常想，為什麼人們能忍受他們所過的這種生活。你或許會將原因歸咎於環境、社會，歸咎於政治組織，但這樣並不能解決問題。我們隨波逐流，過著看起來毫無意義的生活：從早到晚待在辦公室裡，待上五十年甚至更久，然後退休，走向墳墓。當你看到生活中所有不同尋常的美，看到人類在科技領域所取得的偉大成就之後，就會想到為什麼自己的生命中如此缺少美。這裡所說的「美」非指外表的美或外在的裝飾，而是指與大自然默契交流的品質。

人若是與自然失去了聯結，也就失去了與其他人之間的聯結。譬如說讀詩，如果願意的話你可以去讀所有優美的十四行詩，可以聆聽他人朗誦美妙的愛情詩，但美並不存在於對文字的想像之中。空中雲朵、雲中光象、旱路濕地、枝頭小鳥……我們之所以很少看到或欣賞到這些美好的事物，是因為早已被自己的問題、煩惱、莫名的想法和依戀佔據了內在，我們從來都不曾自由過。而美卻是自由者才擁有的特質（這種自由是與獨立完全不同的）。

我想知道，你是如何理解我所說的這一切。如果對於可愛的小狗、路邊的小石或飄浮的孤雲都視若無睹，也沒有半點欣賞之情，如果根本不曾想過去了解世間種種不同尋常的美，那麼我們就會變得渺小而平庸，就是在浪費生命，而完全錯過了生活的美與奧妙。

我們必須回到現實，而現實也是一種真實，一種不平凡的真實。樹枝、暗影、葉片上的光以及空中的鸚鵡都是真實的、實實在在的。從搖曳的棕櫚樹到對於生命的所有感知，當我們理解了所有這些事物的內涵之後，就會形成關於美的超凡意識。但我擔心大家對此興趣寥寥。人們只是傾聽，然後就任由美從身邊溜走。這聽起來或許有些浪漫甚至傷感，但美可不是浪漫、傷感或情緒化的。美是非常、非常堅實的，就像激流中的岩石一樣。

我們必須尋找秩序，因爲我們的生活是無序、混亂而充滿矛盾的。簡而言之，有矛盾、困惑和衝突的地方，必不存在秩序。我們的生活，就這樣日復一日地，充滿了矛盾、混亂、衝突和欺騙。這是事實。你或許曾想過能否把秩序帶到這種混亂中，因爲沒有秩序就沒有效率。但你應先明瞭的是，秩序與情感、浪漫毫無關係，它是連續性的、邏輯嚴謹而完整的。

那麼，我們能不能擁有秩序？它並非紙上藍圖，亦非基於傳統或是由某位大師、領袖制定的，與我們自身的欲望和衝動也毫無關聯——而是指一種持續存在的秩序。我們如何才能夠把秩序帶到自己的生活中，以消除二元對立、矛盾和欺騙——不管是在政治上、宗教上還是與他人關係上的？我們經常會產生幻想，認爲自己已經進入了冥想狀態，但如果日常生活中沒有秩序，那麼不管是在做什麼，都不可能是冥想。因此，我們必須奠定冥想的基礎，也就是秩序。

首先，我們要明白自己的日常生活究竟有多混亂。這裡並不是在探討如何把秩序帶到無序中，而是強調要理解無序的本質。只有理解了無序的本質，才能感受到秩序的美。這種秩序並不是要強加給自己、強制而爲之的，也不等同于遵守傳統習俗。只要你眞正探究清楚無序的特質，秩序自然就會出現。所以，你儘管去做吧！

人類具有超強的能力，可以在科技領域取得巨大成就。人類擁有非凡的想像力，幾乎創造出了所有的概念、原則、觀念和宗教神明，發明了各種各樣的宗教儀式，有的甚至可以用美輪美奐來形容，但都毫無意義。實際上，人類的頭腦具有偉大的品質。它不僅包括各種形式的感官活動，而且還具備各種官能，如愛、關懷、關注、尋求智慧的能力和博愛意識。所有這一切構成了完整的頭腦。說到這兒，你會想要更進一步提出質疑，好讓頭腦充分發揮其功能嗎？因爲，沒有質疑的生活就是無序的。

你應該質疑的是，這麼多個世紀以來，爲什麼人類一直坦然接受無序的生活——不論是在政治上、宗教上、經濟上、社會上，還是在人際關係上？爲什麼？爲什麼我們會接受這種生活方式？你期望去哪里尋找答案？既然提出質疑，你就要竭盡所能尋找答案。在這裡，我要對你提出質疑：請充分運用你的能力，全力以赴，看看有無可能在一個退化、墮落、不道德的世界裡過上健全、完整的生活。這是我對你的挑戰與質疑。你對此作何反應？「完整」一詞意味著健康——包括生理上的和心理上的，其中心理上的健康就是指要具備心的所有能力，即所謂的心智健全。此外，「完整」還有神聖、莊嚴之意。只有具備這些品質，生活才是完整的。

身爲人類的你是否覺察到，自己以及周圍的整個世界已是完全混亂、不斷退化著？這裡所說的「覺察」，不是想像或假設，而是指看到真實存在、正在發生的事，如政治、宗教、社會的道德退化。沒有任何機構、宗教導師或準則倫理可以阻止這種退化。它正在全世界範圍內發生著。

你覺察到了嗎？如果覺察到了，又該怎麼應對？該採取什麼行動？我是指當下該如何行動，而不是在問將來。我們是應該逃避現實，無視世界的退化，還是聯合起來，一同調查、探究其中根源？

我們應該怎麼做？在我看來，首先需要正視自己的生活，正視現實，正視生活中正在發生的事，因爲我們的生活即是社會，你無法改變自己的生活。這是顯而易見的事實。共產主義者、無政府主義者、社會主義者都無法改變它。誦讀《薄伽梵歌》或《奧義書》也無法改變它。篤信佛教或禪宗同樣無用。所有這些都沒有用。那麼，讓我們看一下自己的生活中到底發生了什麼。

我們的日常生活是建立在關係之上的。沒有了關係，你就不可能存在。那麼，你與其他人的關係如何？你與妻子或丈夫、你的老闆、工友或鄰居的關係如何？這種關係中有無秩序，是否只存在以自我爲中心的各種對抗？

這樣的提問，其實是自相矛盾的。假如我已經結婚成家、兒女繞膝、性生活美滿……而如果我以自我爲中心，只關心自己的成功，在乎自己的野心、地位與煩惱，而我的妻子也只關心她自己的煩惱、美貌，那麼兩人之間又怎麼會存在關係呢？如果你有一種信仰，而對方有另外一種信仰或另外一個結論與信條，那麼你們之間就不會存在關係。你沒有注意到這些嗎？我們有無可能將秩序帶到你與妻子或丈夫的關係中，而不是你與天地、宇宙、神明的關係中？所謂神明，是思想的產物。你可以與思想發明的這些事物保持非同尋常的關係，但那只是幻覺。與妻子（丈夫）以及子女保持好關係才是重要的,唯有如此,衝突才會消弭,秩序才會顯現。

那麼,你現在如何才能造就秩序?秩序即是空無中的序列,而空無存於心間。這意味著人的心智永遠都不會被任何煩惱佔據。然而,如今我們的心智已被各種信仰、追求、困惑和幻想塞得滿滿當當,不再有任何空閒之地。這樣一來,也就不會形成秩序。而如果日常生活中沒有秩序,那麼你的冥想就只是對現實生活的逃避。而這種帶有逃避性質的冥想只會導致幻想。

因此,你必須明確冥想的基礎,去尋求不可測度、不可言喻的超越了思想的秩序。不過,唯有在全然自由的情況下,你才可能理解秩序,也才能尋得那超越思想的秩序的存在之所。

第七章 | 專 注

專注意味著不僅用耳朵去聽，
而且還要用心去聽。
專注還意味著去看、去觀察——
不僅用眼睛，而且還要用心。
專注也意味著學習。
觀察、傾聽、學習，
這三者都是專注的內涵。

大多數人的生活都已經被片段化，分割成了商務生活、宗教生活、家庭生活、性生活，等等。所有人都不是完整的，總是通過某一個特別的視角、結論或某種理想化的觀念看待自己的生活。這樣的觀察全都是片面的。我們能否從完全不同的另一個角度看待問題？如果已經意識到自己正被片段化，生活已變得支離破碎、充滿各種矛盾與對峙，那我們還有無可能換一個角度來看待問題？

生活中存在各種各樣的問題，而且在這樣一個高度發達、異常複雜、人口過多的社會裡，問題正在不斷增加。解決了一個問題之後，我們或許又創造了其他更多的問題。為什麼會這樣？如果不依靠早已習慣了解決問題的大腦，我們有無可能解決問題？

讓我們看看吧。我們五六歲就開始上學，而且在孩提時代就面臨著諸多問題：要學習如何讀、寫，還要學習數學。從那時起，我們的大腦就已經習慣了解決問題。而當上了大學之後，又會遇到新的問題。大學畢業之後，工作、個人發展、職業選擇等問題接踵而至，充塞著我們的大腦。

我們總是從一個已經習慣去解決問題的大腦那裡尋求解決之道。可是如果大腦已經被問題佔據了所有空間，它又怎麼能夠解決問題呢？

自幼時起，我們的大腦就已經習慣了去解決一個又一個的問題。因此，它甚至不先去理解問題本身，而只是尋求解決方法。我們有無可能擁有一個沒有這種習慣的大腦？

如今我們的大腦已經習慣了解決問題，但實際上問題越來越多，從不曾被解決過。為什麼？是因為大腦從未努力過嗎？我們有無可能擁有一個可以真正瞭解問題本質的大腦？在理解上述這些問題的過程中，你可能會發現，解決方法就藏在問題之中。

舉一個非常普通的例子。我們從未停止過戰爭，自人類在地球上誕生以來，戰爭就持續不斷。我們從未解決過戰爭這個問題，只是想著如何才能進行更滿意的屠殺，而這就是所謂的進步。我不是在說笑話。人們建立了一個又一個組織，先是國際聯盟，亦即通常所說的國聯，現在又有聯合國，但戰爭仍在繼續。我們從一個組織轉到另一個組織，希望能夠通過它們解決問題。然而，問題非但沒有得到解決，而且還變得越來越多。戰爭從未停止。

戰爭的根源是民族主義、經濟分歧、地域分歧。語言、種族、宗教、經濟和文化上的分歧將我們分割開來。雖然同是人類，同樣都受苦受難，都有痛苦和渴望，都會感到厭煩、孤獨和絕望。但我們對此並不關心，而只是想解決那些看似由外因而起的問題。

　　自童年起就已習慣去解決問題的大腦能否擺脫各種束縛，自由地面對問題？你會這樣做嗎？這是個問題。你是否意識到，自生命誕生時起，人類的大腦就一直在與各式各樣的問題作鬥爭，並試圖找到答案？可是，只有當我們認識到大腦受束縛的時候，才能找到正確的答案，而只要大腦一如既往地習慣於解決問題，那我們將永遠都不會找到解決辦法。

　　有些人如果與妻子關係不睦，就會離婚、再婚，一直如此反復。他若是擁有大量的時間和精力，自然可以樂此不疲地進行下去。但解決問題的關鍵不在於離婚，也與關係的複雜性無關，而是要深入理解關係的意義。關係是我們生命中最重要的事之一，但這裡所說的是深層次的關係，與大發脾氣或神經兮兮等情緒上的表現無關。然而，我們對此從來都沒有探尋過。雖然我們希望解決關係的問題，但其實永遠都不可能解決；雖然這個世界上的精神病醫生和心理醫生越來越多，但他們也解決不了深層次的關係問題。

　　我們應該一同探討生活的藝術。什麼是生活的藝術？我們熟悉詩歌、繪畫、烹飪等藝術，卻從來沒有問過自己「什麼是生活的藝術」——而這或許是最偉大的藝術之一。也許你會問：「生活中有藝術嗎？還是說，生活中只有幾率，比如遺傳學幾率、生物學幾率？」如果你非要提出這類問題，那麼藝術也就不復存在了。

讓我們一起探尋什麼是生活的藝術吧——這裡所說的是廣義和深層含義上的「藝術」，而不只是指博物館裡的藝術收藏品。如果有人問你什麼是生活的藝術，你會如何回答？

不過，無論是思索後做出的回答，還是帶有個人色彩、情緒化或理想式的回答，都毫無意義。不是嗎？如果我給出一個情緒化的答案：「生活的藝術就是最高的願望」，或者「生活的藝術就是最崇高的智慧」，這種回答其實沒有任何意義，而且非常片面。也許你還會說，生活的藝術是對生命的全面展望，這聽起來很不錯，但也不對。

那麼，到底什麼是生活的藝術呢？顯然它是指生活中沒有任何衝突。一個時時都處於衝突狀態、時時都有問題、都以自我為中心的大腦，必然是存在局限的。比如說，如果一個人正在想著自己的事情，那又怎麼可能是在冥想，因為這時你所謂的冥想是以自我為中心的。所以，生活的藝術指的就是過著沒有衝突的生活。

這有沒有可能呢？生活中總是存在著二元性，即必有一物克制另一物。只要人的意識仍是以自我為中心，那他的生活中就必然有衝突，因為這種以自我為中心的意識是狹隘、渺小的，而且微不足道。當然，即便你知道了這些，但仍可以我行我素。你會說，現代社會的人們在生活中多多少少都會以自我爲中心。那麼，你可曾試過？你可曾試過不再以自我爲中心，不再只想著你自己，即便只是一天，甚至只是一個小時？然後，你看一看會發生什麼吧。你會發現自己完全不受約束了！隨後，你也可以重新回到以自我爲中心的生活——顯然這才是人類的生活常態，沒有人會對你說三道四。因此，你就去嘗試一個小時不再想著自己吧。如果能夠堅持一個小時，那你也可以堅持更長的時間。而這種不以自我爲中心的生活將會給予你巨大的能量與激情，去追求更具深遠意義的目標。

　　什麼是專注？它是一種身體行爲嗎？它是思想的運動嗎？是因欲望（即意志力的本質）而採取的行動嗎？人們如何保持專注力？它是自然出現的嗎？人們是否無需付出巨大努力，無需上大學或接受宗教導師的訓導就可以形成專注力？現在，讓我們來探討這個問題（但不是爲了尋求答案）。

　　專注意味著不僅用耳朵去聽，而且用心去聽。專注還意味著去看、去觀察——不僅用眼睛，而且還要用心。專注還意味著學習。觀察、傾聽、學習，這三者都是專注的內涵。

　　什麼是學習？學習是記憶嗎？就如同我們上學（包括上大學）

時所必需的那種記憶？上學的時候，我們不停地記憶，將書本上的知識以及專家、老師和舍監傳授的知識存儲起來。這就是學習嗎？我們總是不停地積累、運用知識，而不管熟練與否。對於木匠大師的學徒來說，他要學習的是瞭解木材的品質、種類、紋理，以及是否美觀、觸感如何、怎樣運用，等等。他是在通過日復一日、月復一月的木工知識與實踐經驗的積累，來進行我們所謂的學習。而這種學習顯然很有限，因為不管過去還是將來的所有知識都是有限的。

那麼，有沒有一種學習方式是不受限的？有沒有一種學習不是通過知識積累，而是通過傾聽（包括傾聽時對對方言語的反應，如對特定詞「愛」和「恨」的反應）和觀察（不帶任何偏見、不受任何思想影響）實現的？在看一棵樹的時候，你能不能做到心中無「樹」？你有沒有這樣做過？這意味著不帶預設觀點與動機地觀察，而且不受他人思想的影響。這樣的學習，是一個永無止境的過程。

因此，保持專注便十分必要。專注的初始即是開始覺察之時。此刻坐在這裡，我們能否在靜默中細察周圍的所有事物？然而覺察之後，我們便會開始選擇：那件藍色襯衫不錯，比我穿的這件好多了；你的髮型比我的好看多了，等等。我們總是在比較、判斷、評估，而所有這些行為都是選擇。我們是否可以不做選擇，只是覺察？

你可以做到嗎？如果可以，那麼你就會發現這種專注的覺察與關注是完全不同的。關注是將所有的思想都集中到某個特定的主題、書頁或單詞上面。這樣的關注意味著要切斷、排斥其他所有的思想，因而必然帶有局限性。但我們在做某件事情的時候，又不得不集中注意力。例如清洗餐具時，就得小心翼翼以免將其打碎，同時要使用合適的清潔劑以及足夠乾淨的水。

但你應當明白，做這些事所需要的也就是不加選擇地專注其上。即是說，不去關注，不加判斷、評估、批評和比較地去覺察。這就是自然地保持專注。

當我聽你講故事，聽到動人心弦的情節時，就會十分認真地去聽。當你告訴我某件非常、非常嚴肅的事情時，我也會全神貫注地傾聽、理解你所說的話。也許我心中另有所想，但全部的注意力仍然在你那兒。這時的我便是全然專注的——我的整個人甚至體內的每一根神經都在試圖理解你所說的話。

在這樣的專注中，「我」已經不存在了。明白嗎？在保持完全的專注時，我把所有的精力都用於理解對方所說的話，而不再想著「我」自己。因此在內心深處，也就不會有「我必須注意聽」的想法存在。

第八章 | 不再恐懼

人們追本溯源，
分析恐懼背後的成因。
它的成因或許有一百個，又或許只有一個。
而一種恐懼的結果又會成爲導致另一種恐懼的原因。
由此，因果相生，迴圈不息。
所以，當你探求恐懼的緣由時，
就會被束縛在這樣的困境中，
永遠無從解脫。

我將要探討一個全新的問題，希望你們能夠認真、嚴肅地聽。不管你是否同意我的看法，我都希望能夠帶動大家一起進行充滿邏輯、周詳、理性而且謙卑的思考。

技能在我們的生命中已經變得至關重要，各所大學、專科院校以及各級中小學校的教育無不以此為導向。如果一個人所受的教育完全是以學習技能為目的，那麼他將不可避免地由此養成權力意識，變得傲慢和自大。那麼，技能和明性之間有什麼關係呢？明性和憐憫之間的關係又是如何呢？

我們經常談論傾聽、觀察和學習的藝術。所謂傾聽的藝術，就是自然地去傾聽，讓所有的事物都置於合適的位置。「藝術」一詞的含義就是讓事物各就其位，各歸其所。

而觀察的藝術，就在於毫無歪曲。若想要在觀察的感知中獲得超常的明性，那麼必不可有任何歪曲，否則便不能算是觀察了。而你不論是帶著何種形式的動機、目的或方向去觀察，都會導致歪曲。

學習的藝術並不僅僅在於知識的積累 —— 雖然這對於熟練掌握技能來說十分必要，但避免累積性地去學習同樣重要。學習形式通常有兩種：一種是通過經驗傳承、書本介紹和學校教育來獲取、積累知識，依據大腦中存儲的知識去行動，而不管是否已經熟練掌握那些知識；另一種是從不積累知識，你完全明白哪些知識是絕對必須掌握，哪些又是毫無意義的，並且只記住那些有必要記住的知識。這樣一來，大腦就不會因為太多知識的擁塞而一直處於混亂狀態。

　　所以，喚醒智慧需要三個基本條件：掌握沒有任何歪曲的傾聽藝術，準確地進行口頭與非口頭的表達和交流；掌握不預設任何方向、動機和目的的觀察藝術，去做清晰、純粹的觀察；還要掌握學習的藝術，積累所有有助於熟練掌握技能的必要知識，摒棄任何的心理反射或回應，讓大腦只在必要的時候熟練發揮其功用和技能。

　　不過，想要完全明白哪些知識絕對必要，哪些毫無意義，並只記錄那些有必要記住的知識，其實非常困難。例如有人侮辱你或是恭維你，有人對你指指點點、說三道四，這些都是不需要大腦記錄的無用資訊。這樣一來，你就不會從心理上形成「小我」的自我架構。只有當你開始記錄那些毫無意義的事，即看重一個人的姓名、外貌、經驗、看法和結論時，才會形成那樣的自我架構，造成對真相的歪曲。

　　如果你不附帶任何結論或看法 —— 它們都是造成歪曲的肇因 —— 去傾聽，便可以毫不費力地發現真相，因為你是全神貫注地去傾聽，因而摒棄了所有虛假的資訊。而當你帶著結論、看法、信條或信仰去觀察時，就不可能看得十分清晰。在我們的生命中，學習如何熟練掌握謀生技能固然很有必要，但我們在大腦中所做的許多記錄都是歪曲的，過於強調技能將會導致生活的機械化。

傾聽、觀察和學習的藝術能賦予我們非比尋常的明性，這種明性是可以用語言來交流的。如果沒有明性，那麼掌握技能者就會滋養出自大心理。不管對個人、團體或國家來說，都是如此。很顯然，自大是與明性相斥的。如果沒有憐憫心，那麼你就不可能有明性。而正是因為我們沒有憐憫心，才把技能看得那麼重要。

任何一種恐懼都會排斥明性。許多人都面臨著各種各樣的恐懼，而恐懼與憐憫又是相斥的。任何形式的恐懼，不管是生理上的還是心理上的，都會歪曲明性。因而，只要人心中還存有恐懼，那麼他就不會有憐憫之心。人有各種各樣的恐懼——害怕變老，害怕失去丈夫、妻子或孩子，害怕失敗，等等。恐懼不請自來，只要你還活著，就會感覺到恐懼的存在，它們可能就潛藏在你的潛意識之中。所以，你可以現在就去看看潛意識之中的恐懼情緒。

看的藝術，也就是觀察的藝術，只有在你不再想著如何擺脫恐懼的時候才可能出現。而你只要還在想著如何擺脫恐懼，或是仍然沒有意識到自己的恐懼，就可能導致觀察的歪曲。當然，心底的恐懼再多，也都只有一個根源。就如同一棵樹能生成千枝萬葉一樣，恐懼之樹同樣枝繁葉茂，並由此生出不同的花和果，即我們所說的

「行為」。因此，人必須探求恐懼的最終根源，而非其外在的各種表現形式。

比方說，有的人可能害怕黑暗，有的人卻害怕失去自己的妻子或丈夫，有的人可能害怕沒有錢，有的人害怕的卻是再次遭遇往昔的痛苦，或是害怕別的各種各樣的事。我們可以對這些恐懼情緒一一進行分析，但這會浪費很多時間，不是嗎？而如果找到了恐懼的根源，那一切都會變得簡單明瞭。

我認為很多人並沒有意識到或是真正理解恐懼的本質及其對人類的影響。事實上，只要心底存有恐懼，人就可能因此做出神經質的行為。例如，許多人都覺得孤獨，於是會尋求友誼，以擺脫孤獨。友誼因此變得非常重要，而如果沒有朋友，恐懼就會隨之產生。你也可能為自己建造一堵心的圍牆，以此反抗、逃避孤獨，並因此採取各種不夠明智的行為。因此，理解恐懼的本質和結構就非常重要，因為恐懼與明性總是相斥，而如果沒有明性，那麼就無法喚醒智慧，這對你、對我來說都是一樣。人依照這種智慧所採取的行為，是非機械化的行為，因而也就不存在任何動機。

因此，理解恐懼並不再陷入其中，就非常重要。那麼，不論是否已經意識到恐懼的存在，大家都明瞭將其消除的重要性和急迫性了嗎？對於已經意識到的恐懼，克服起來會相對容易一些，而要想消除那些依然潛藏於內心深處、我們尚不瞭解的恐懼，則困難得多。你將如何探尋那些根深蒂固的恐懼？它們有無可能探尋得到？

心理學家表示，通過分析、夢境解析或心理療法探析，人是有可能克服藏於內心深處的恐懼的。然而，分析並不會讓我們的心變得明淨。分析無法帶來明性，因為你分析得越多，有待分析的就會越多。這或許會花費你一生的時間，最終卻一無所得！

　　讓我們一同來探尋分析的真相——這真相既不是專屬於你的，也不是我的。首先，在分析中有觀察者和被觀察者、分析者與被分析者之分。分析者說：「我要分析我的反應，我的夢想和恐懼。」但分析者與恐懼是否不同？分析者與他即將分析之事是否不同？你必須瞭解這一點。分析者與被分析者是否不同？如果你說他們是不同的，而大多數人也都這樣認為，那麼你就會陷入永無止境的衝突之中。這是因為，在分析者研究、分析他的反應——嫉妒、憤怒、暴力——的過程中，分析者認為他與被分析者是彼此分割、互不相同的。而這種分割必然造成分裂，因而也就會導致衝突。哪里有分裂，哪里就必然有衝突——不論這種分裂是兩個國家之間的還是男女之間的。當然，男性與女性的生理差異不是分裂，從生物學上講，男女之間顯然有別。我們所說的分裂，指的是他們的想法、他們對彼此的累積反應與影像的差異。正因為如此，他們的關係中才會有衝突。

　　因此，哪里有分析，哪里就必然會產生衝突。最為不幸的是，我們已經習慣了衝突，那就是我們的生活方式。如果沒有了衝突，我們會說：「我這是怎麼了？」而神經質的本質便是衝突。

談到分析，還必須提及時間因素。因為分析可能需要數天、數月乃至數年，如果你有足夠的精力、能力和財力，也可以永無休止地分析自己。這是非常有趣的！而後，你還要尋求他人的幫助，陳述自己的問題所在，並為此傾盡所有以求解決問題。這顯然是浪費時間，延誤真正解決問題的時機。你必須看清的事實就是，分析意味著衝突、時間的流逝，更意味著問題永遠無法解決。而明瞭這個真相之後，你就不會再去分析了。

那麼，你還會怎麼做？從心理上講，分析浪費時間，導致衝突，而且任何分析都必須是完整的，不是嗎？否則，你帶著昨日不夠完整的分析成果，去接著分析新的事實，新的分析總會打上過去的烙印。如果你能夠清楚地看到這一點，我也希望知道，你要是不去分析，還會怎麼做？如果你已經發現分析無用，不會帶來任何實質性的結果，那麼你會做什麼？

我們再來探討如何消除恐懼。大多數人都習慣於分析恐懼，分析它的原因與結果。是什麼讓人產生恐懼？人們追本溯源，分析背後的成因。它的成因或許有一百個，又或許只有一個。而一種恐懼的結果又會成為導致另一種恐懼的原因。由此，因果相生，迴圈不息。所以，當你探求恐懼的緣由時，就會被束縛在這樣的困境中，永遠無從解脫。這是分析的真相之一。

於是，有人就會問：「如果不做分析，我的恐懼可以消除嗎？」須知，人或許會有很多種恐懼，但我們只要關注恐懼的根源，而非其「枝葉」。如果你能夠將恐懼連根拔起，就算大功告成了，因為這樣一來，整棵「恐懼之樹」必死無疑。那麼，恐懼的根是什麼？是時間嗎？時間的一種形式是時序時間，即鐘錶上的時間——從日出到日落的一天二十四小時。時間還有另外一種形式，即始終著眼于「明天」的心理時間，譬如我一心想要到後天再去解決問題。因此，恐懼是時間的產物嗎？我在昨天或者上周經歷了一場痛苦，並被大腦記錄下來。當大腦記錄了這段痛苦經歷後，我便擔心下周是否還會經歷這樣的痛苦。而如果大腦中沒有記錄，那麼我就不會產生恐懼。

有量度便有恐懼。當一個人將自己與其他人相比較時，就會感到恐懼：我沒你聰明，我希望和你一樣聰明，但又害怕趕不上你。所有這些其實都是時間的運動，時間本身即是一種量度與比較。因此，量度、時間、比較、模仿就會導致恐懼。而時間、量度、比較，實質上又是思想的運動。因此，思想是恐懼的最終根源。請注意這一推斷的邏輯性。

我們一同思考，一同研究、探索，最終發現，無論是分析，還是探尋恐懼的原因或者時間，都不是解決之道，其中時間只是一個量度、一種比較，是思想的運動。因此可見，解決問題的關鍵並不在於如何消除或者壓制恐懼，而是要理解整個思想的運動。現在，你是不是不再急於消除恐懼？我們正在討論的是一個更宏觀、更詳盡的問題，務必要全面、完整地理解思想的整個運動。須知，只要心中依然存有狹隘、不完整的「小我」，那麼恐懼就仍會生起。

　　學習、觀察和傾聽的藝術中並不存在思想的運動。如果我正在專注地聽你談話，為什麼還要讓思想介入呢？我正在看，正在觀察，這種觀察中同樣不存在思想的運動。我只是觀察，觀察山、樹、河、人，其中並不涉及我的任何背景的投射，而這種背景的投射即是思想的運動。在積累技能知識方面，思想是必要的，但除此之外，思想一無是處。了知這一點，便能產生莫大的明性，不是嗎？

　　我希望你擁有明性。那意味著你的行為沒有焦點，你的思想中不會有諸如「我」、「我的」、「他們」或「我們」這樣的焦點。有焦點的地方必定有圓周，也就必定有抵抗，有分裂，這是恐懼的基本「肇因」之一。

　　因此，當我們思索恐懼的解決之道，也就是在思索思想的整個運動，而正是思想滋生了恐懼。此外，明性只有在思想完全中止的時候才有可能存在；也就是說，彼時思想只在學習知識方面發揮作用，而不進入其他領域，這樣一來，所有的看法、判斷和評估都會完全消除，你只需傾聽、觀察和學習即可。沒有明性，技能就會成為生命中最具破壞力的因素，這也正是當今世界上正在發生的事。你可以登上月球，將國旗插在那裡，但這並不是明性。你可以通過戰爭，運用偉大的科技成就（也就是運用思想）去殺人。你可以將人類劃分為不同的種族、歸入不同的社區，等等，所有這些分裂都是由思想造成的。

思想本身即是分裂的。它狹隘、有局限性，因為它是以經驗、記憶和知識為基礎，而經驗、記憶和知識都是過去的，與時間捆綁在一起。但只要是帶有時間性的，也必然是有限的，所以說思想有局限性。因此，我們永遠無法依據思想來理解何為完整，何為無遠弗屆與永恆。思想當然可以創造出各種想像中的未來，可以去想像那種永恆與無遠弗屆，但它仍是有局限的。因此，思想創造的「上帝」也是有局限的。我擔心你們當中信仰上帝的人不明白這一點，因為上帝其實就是思想的產物，是內在恐懼、安全感缺失的產物。

只要明白了這一點，明性就會像撥雲見日一樣出現在你的面前。要知道，思想即是言語，而言語絕非事物。言語是對事物的描述，卻不等於事物本身。既然如此，恐懼也就毫無必要。此外，你還必須清楚思想是否仍處於它所應在的領域，而未擅入他處。

記錄是大腦的功能。在知識領域，這種記錄是安全、可靠的。否則你就無法生存。人必須要有衣服穿、有飯吃、有房子住，而只有當思想安處其位，即只在知識領域發揮作用時，這才有可能實現。如此一來，大腦不會再做多餘的記錄，可以自由地去看、去觀察，而國與國、「你」與「我」之間的分裂或區別也就不復存在。

有了明性，技能就不再是機械化的，因為無論何種技能，都正是因為有明性它才得以發揮本有的作用，明性則源於憐憫之心。因此，我們必須從深層次探究何為憐憫。此前，我們已經非常清楚地談論了明性和技能，以及沒有明性的技能的危險性。這其中涉及三者，即憐憫、明性和技能。而只要有憐憫，明性和技能就不會分裂，憐憫即是一種運動。只是我們被技能所束縛，以致看不到它的整個運動。

憐憫的本質和結構是什麼？我們必須看清有關快樂、愛、苦難和死亡的全部問題，才能瞭解這一點。你不能簡單地說，「我有憐憫。」這並不代表你真的憐憫。就好像一個人說「我很聰明」，並不代表他就很聰明，因為那只是一種自我意識。只要有自我意識存在，智慧就不可能存在。

要想瞭解憐憫的美，及其深度、重要性和意義，我們不僅要探究恐懼，而且還要理解快樂。愛是快樂嗎？是欲望嗎？是另外一種記憶或影像嗎？思考憐憫的問題時，就會涉及所有這些。而只有當我們團結起來，才能夠弄明白這些問題。因為個體並不孤單，整個人類的本質都體現在個人身上。這是事實，也是現實。這並不是我的發明，也不是為了表示自己比別人聰明而這麼說。

一個確鑿無疑的事實是，作為人類的一分子，你其實已經生活了數千年，你就是整個人類的代表，人類所受的苦難、所流的淚、所受的屠戮，以及人類的妒忌、憤怒、憂慮、快樂、恐懼，等等這些全都體現在你的身上。你就是這所有的一切。因而，你也就是整個人類。倘若在你的意識中發生了某種全面性的革命，那麼這場革命就會波及所有人類的意識。這是事實。我們之所以要視之為重要而急迫的問題，要非常認真、嚴肅地去探討，原因就在於此。當你從根源上去解決這件事情，因而改變了意識的內容時，那麼你就影響了全人類。

第九章 ｜ 喚醒所有的感覺

爲什麼我們從未運用自己的全部感知去瞭解事物，
尤其是在看一棵樹、
一座山或一片海的時候？
這難道不是因爲我們一直以來都過著
充滿紛爭的生活，
生活在有限的空間裡嗎？

什麼是美？美是依據某項原則、某種特定的規則來判定的嗎？或者，根據關注程度的不同，會看到完全不同的美？

當我們看到起伏的山巒、夜晚的天空，看到晨光灑向大地，就會陷入極度的靜默。你只是靜靜地看著，在你與自然景色之間，還存在著巨大的空間距離。當你看到令人歎為觀止的高山，看到皚皚雪山與藍天交相輝映的一瞬間，高山的那種美麗、壯觀與雄偉，會讓你變得全然靜寂。這是美所帶來的震撼力。極其美妙的景致，壯觀的高山與深谷，會在瞬間驅散你的所有疑惑。自我懷疑、焦慮擔憂、自言自語，這些都將不復存在；也沒有一個實體，沒有自我，沒有「我」在觀看。當自我不存在時，就會出現無與倫比的美。

藝術在我們的生命中扮演什麼角色？為什麼任何事物都應該在我們的生命中扮演一種角色？依我看來，最偉大的藝術即生活的藝術，而非繪畫、雕塑、詩歌或偉大的文學作品。這些藝術作品的地位與成就當然無可爭議，但就個人而言，生活的藝術才是最偉大的藝術。因爲它超越了生命中的任何角色。

　　美學是一種感知能力，一種覺察能力，意味著人必須具備敏銳的覺察力，而敏銳與否取決於靜默的程度深淺。這種敏銳並不是大學裡可以學到的，也不是可以讓別人教給你的。如果不能保持一定的靜默，你就無法敏銳覺察。譬如，當你靜靜地看一片樹林，你們之間就會產生交流，這是與自然的溝通和交融。只是，我們大多數人都已經失去了與自然的聯結——包括樹木、高山，乃至地球上的所有生物。

　　就我們的人際關係而言，敏銳是指意識到彼此的存在。這可能嗎？生活的藝術是找到一種沒有衝突的關係，彼此和諧相處，沒有爭吵，沒有佔有與被佔有，不再害怕孤獨——這一切都是人類一直在抗拒的。而生存的藝術遠比那些偉大畫家的藝術更重要。不過，聽音樂、參觀世界上的各種博物館並對此津津樂道、閱讀藝術書籍——這些或許可以讓我們得以暫時逃避自己的問題、焦慮和憂傷吧。

　　我們能不能過一種具有深刻美學感知的生活，從而理解何爲言語何爲噪音，並明瞭人類究竟有多庸俗？與嘈雜的環境相比，人在安靜的環境中可以學到更多知識。這聽起來真像老生常談，但實則不然。因爲你在保持安靜的同時，還需要去做大量的觀察。而這種觀察與任何形式的權威都是相抵觸的，比如說尋求他人的幫助，讓他們指導你如何觀察。你應按照自己的方式，只是觀察，並且不受任何噪音的干擾。這便是生活的藝術。

正如前面說過的，所謂藝術，就是將萬物放到合適的位置，讓它們和諧共生；就是去觀察內心深處的矛盾——人的欲望通常很強烈，但你要觀察這一切而不是去製造對立，要單純地觀察真相並接受它。這或許是讓生活更加和諧的一種方式。

我希望你看山，而不是看我。作為演講者的我其實並不重要。而無論我說的話重要與否，你都必須自己去發現。

生命中什麼才是重要的？生命的根本或基本要素是什麼？現在各種電視節目、文學作品和雜誌越來越多，但所有這一切都如過眼雲煙。如果陷入困境，你會尋求專業人士的幫助，而他們給出的答案只會越來越膚淺，給出答案的時間也越來越短。一切都變得那麼膚淺、低俗、幼稚。當然，這裡的「低俗」一詞並無不敬或冒犯之意。

你可能從來都沒有問過生命中的基本問題或基本要求是什麼。當然，這個問題與任何信仰、信條、信念，或者其他種種看似睿智的廢話都沒有關係。無論共產主義思想或天主教神學，無論是馬克思、列寧還是聖托馬斯・阿奎那①的思想，它們都是一樣的，都屬

---

①聖托馬斯・阿奎那：中世紀哲學家、神學家，被天主教教會論定為歷史上最偉大的神學家。

於信仰、信念、信條、宗教理論、結論和意識形態。但相對我們的生命而言，所有這些都是膚淺的。實際上任何事物都是如此。

我們擁有五花八門的娛樂設施、宗教信仰和足球賽事，讓人陶醉其中，為之大聲喝彩、吶喊，卻從不曾靜默相對或安靜地觀察。那麼，在我們的生命中，什麼是最基本卻又最重要的？

思想能夠覺察到它本身嗎？思想創造了一個與它本身分離的思想者。思想者說：「我必須覺察到自己所想的，我必須控制自己的思想，絕不能將其丟失。」而思想者是基於思想來行動的。那麼，思想者與思想有何不同？換言之，是思想創造了思想者還是思想者創造了思想？在這個世界上，如果沒有思想，那麼就沒有思想者。

事實上，更重要的事情是找出以下因素之間存在二元性、存在對立與矛盾的原因：「我」和思想，作為思想者的「我」，見證者，觀察者以及被觀察的事物。我們可以認為是思想者在控制、塑造思想，將它塑造成自己想要的樣子。但問題是，思想者與思想有區別嗎？有沒有哪種思想不是由思想者創造出來的？

讓我們看一下其中的邏輯。從字面意義和理智上判斷，我們可以非常清楚地看到思想者與思想的區別，而且是先有思想，才出現

中世紀哲學家

思想者。因此，思想者即是過去，他的記憶與知識都是屬於過去的，因爲它們皆源自於思想，而思想又來自於經驗。因此，思想者的所有活動都是過去的。於是我們就會說：「思想與作爲思想者的我是不一樣的。」我們很快便從邏輯、智慧的層面上接受了這一說法。但爲什麼說是在智慧的層面上理解了？這難道不是因爲我們並沒有從整體上去觀察嗎？我們只是從智慧的角度去看待某個事物。爲什麼會這樣？是因爲我們大多數人的智慧高度發達嗎，還是因爲我們的智慧比敏感性、直接感知力更發達？

實際上，之所以出現這種情況，是因爲我們自孩提時代起就被訓練著去接受、去記憶，運用大腦去存儲那些別人告訴我們的事，久而久之養成了習慣。因此，當遇到新事物時，我們會說，「我在智慧層面上理解了。」我們並沒有從整體上去全面瞭解這個新事物，並沒有喚醒自己所有的感覺。我們從未完全地接受它，從未全面地觀察一個事物，只會說：「是的，這符合邏輯。」然後便頓足不前，不再追問爲什麼只有「智慧」這部分的感覺被喚醒。

智慧感知只是部分敏感性與知覺發揮作用的結果。比如說製造一台電腦，你通常只會從智慧的層面進行思考，而沒有揮發出所有的激情和感覺。這種情形已經演化成爲一種機械性的運動，而你一直在重複這種機械性。因此，當你看到新事物時，就會機械地用老方法對待：只是在智慧層面上去理解，卻沒有完全瞭解它。也就是說，你並沒有全然領悟。

爲什麽我們從未運用自己的全部感知去瞭解事物，尤其是在看一棵樹、一座山或一片海的時候？這難道不是因爲我們一直以來都過著分離的生活，生活在有限的空間裡嗎？事實正是如此。

　　因此，去看吧，運用你所有的感官去看。當你運用所有的感官，比如眼睛、耳朵、神經時，當你運用整個大腦去反應時，在觀察過程中就不會存在「我」這個焦點。

　　我們要問的是思想能否覺察到它本身。這個問題異常複雜，需要進行仔細的觀察。思想通過民族主義、宗教派系之間的衝突創造了戰爭。思想創造了這一切。上帝並未創造教會體制，並未創造出主教和各種各樣的禮袍和儀式，也沒有創造形形色色的香和蠟燭。教堂裡的所有一切都源於思想，源于古人——古埃及人、古印度人、古希伯來人等等，是他們思想的拷貝。所有的這一切都與思想有關。因此，「上帝」其實也是由思想創造出來的。

　　有沒有人對死亡與生存毫無畏懼？有沒有人認爲自己的生活毫無問題，不需要信仰上帝？讓我們仔細看看思想所發揮的作用。思想可以覺察到它自身的作爲，因此思想者和思想之間、觀察者和被觀察者之間並不存在衝突。沒有衝突，也就無需努力。只有當存在衝突與分裂時，人們才會努力解決問題。

　　因此，想要知道人們有無可能過上一種無需任何努力、沒有任何衝突的生活，我們必須先瞭解清楚思想的整個運動軌跡。但有些人會說他沒有時間或是不願意去瞭解，因爲他非常繁忙，手頭有很多事要處理。但當他想打高爾夫球時，卻總能找到很多時間。想要瞭解思想的活動，就要對它進行觀察，這是冥想的一部分。

你有沒有探究過什麼是靜默？什麼是靜默？什麼是和平？兩次戰爭之間的間歇是和平嗎？我們是這樣認爲的。我們稱兩次戰爭之間的那段時間爲和平時期。而這一次的戰爭，同下一次戰爭一樣，都是爲結束所有戰爭而發起的。那麼，兩次噪音之間的間歇是和平嗎？兩次吵架之間的間歇是和平嗎？

那什麼是靜默呢？商場或藥店裡都買不到靜默。如果能夠在那兒買到，我們當然會立即去購買。但靜默或者和平都是無法買到的。既然如此，那麼什麼是靜默呢？

靜默必定意味著空間的存在，不是嗎？我可以非常安靜地待在一個狹小的空間內，閉上眼睛，並在身邊壘起一道牆，把自己封閉起來，把注意力集中到日常瑣事上，從中獲得某種程度的和平與安寧。我可以去自己的休息室、書房或靜修室裡坐著，但空間仍然是有限的。這並不僅僅是指房間的大小，也指我的大腦空間非常、非常有限。可大多數人甚至從未問過或是想過這個問題。

那麼，什麼是空間？空間是指從一個點到另一個點嗎？是一個有限的維度嗎？或者，空間裡沒有中心，因而也就沒有邊界？

只要我還看重「我」，在乎「我的問題」、「我的需求」、「我的……」，那麼這就是局限性。而有局限性的空間就是狹小的。但這個狹小空間只是我們為了保護自我而設立的一堵牆，這樣就可以不受打擾，不用擔心遇到問題和麻煩。對大多數人來說，那就是自身擁有的唯一空間。而現在，我們正在這樣的空間裡，問什麼是空間。

存在局限性的空間不會太大。事實就是這樣。而空間意味著靜默。噪音與空間是相排斥的。只要有噪音，空間就不可能存在，不管這種噪音是來自於城鎮生活、人際溝通還是現代音樂。無論噪音是悅耳還是刺耳，有聲音的地方都不可能是靜默的。那麼，擁有足夠的空間意味著什麼？鋼琴上兩個鍵之間的距離是非常小的。兩個人的兩次爭吵間歇的那種靜默，也是一個非常有限的空間。

是否有無限的空間存在？這裡問的不是在天上、宇宙中的空間，而是指在我們的心中、我們的整個生活方式中，是否有真正的、真實而非虛無幻象的巨大空間存在？你可能會說：「嗯，我在智慧層面上能理解這個問題。」但你還要運用所有的感覺，去全面地理解。然後你就會發現，如果真的存在那樣一個巨大的空間，那麼它必定同宇宙有關。

　　對任何人來說，學習都是永無止境的。從書本中學到的是有限的，所有的知識都有其局限性。我們所掌握的有關任何事物的知識也都是有限的，即便科學家也承認這一點。從外界學習知識固然必要，但向內在探尋同樣重要。古希臘人和他們的祖先，就曾經說過要「認識你自己」。這並不意味著你要通過他人來瞭解自己，而是要觀察自己所做的事情，觀察自己的想法、行為、言語、手勢、談話方式、飲食方式等。要觀察，不是修正！不用指出這是對的或那是錯的，只要純粹地觀察。

　　觀察之時，必是靜默的。這樣的觀察就是一種學習，你在學習的同時又是老師。因此，你既是老師又是學生，而不是其他什麼人。學習的過程中，沒有人可以給予你幫助，你只能依靠內在的誠實正直，謙虛向學。

第十章 | 愛、自由、良善與美麗

哪裡有愛，哪裡就有智慧，
而這種智慧並非源於思想，
它是獨立於大腦之外的。
憐憫、愛、自由都是獨立於大腦之外的。
因爲大腦有局限性，它無法包容它們。

大多數人可能很少去探究什麼是生命的本質，以及如何在日常生活中應對醜陋混亂的現象、已逝的快樂和相當多娛樂活動──不管是宗教意義上還是世俗生活裡的娛樂。我們學習專業知識，歷經數年成爲一名醫生或工程師，卻從未問過如何才能過上沒有任何衝突與問題的日常生活。我們一直在努力，一直在掙扎著前行，而當這個問題或挑戰擺在面前時，我們會說：「嗯，雖然這聽起來很不錯，但請告訴我該如何去做，運用何種方式和方法，才能過上安寧和充滿驚奇與美麗的生活？」

應該將「如何」一詞從大腦中清除，在心靈的世界裡（不是學術領域），我們絕不用問「如何」，也絕無必要向任何人──即便是最尊敬的人──問「如何」。他們只會提供給你某種方式或方法，成爲新的束縛，讓你深陷另一種困境。

我們已經談論過戰爭，談論過人類是如何受父母、學校和家庭的束縛。我們都受過心理上的傷害，而這種傷害無疑會滋生恐懼。

關於恐懼，我們已經談了很多。關於時間，我們也已經做了不少討論，而這種時間並不僅僅是指時鐘上的時序時間，還意味著為達成某種成就而定的心理時間。「我現在是這樣，我想成為那樣。」或者：「我很暴力，但將來我會變得不再暴力。」這種從「是什麼」到「要變成什麼」的持續轉變也是時間的要素之一。時間對我們每一個人來說都很重要，它不僅指物理意義上從此地到彼地所需的時間，也指實現思想中所謂的達成理想需要的時間。因此，我們與時間是緊密相連的。像作家以及其他許多人都曾探討過時間有無終點、會不會停止的問題。

請記住，我們是在深入、嚴肅、認真地討論如何過上一種堪稱偉大藝術的生活。現在，讓我們繼續探討。謙虛對於學習而言是必要的，不是嗎？當然，謙虛不是要你卑躬屈膝、不加揀擇地接受，如果那樣就不是謙虛，而只是對權威的認同與崇拜。對於你所尊重的人，也不適用謙虛的態度。而我們大多數人還不具備謙虛的品質。

若要理解異常複雜的生存與自由，就必須謙虛。在許多人看來，所謂自由，就是可以做想做的事，而且事事如意。這個社會的架構之一就是讓每個人都可以自由地去做想做的事情。你可以始終如此自由。無論是想要變得富有，還是希望能夠表達自我，或是冀求特立獨行，你都可以選擇，並將之視為「自由」。於是，人人都想要表達自己的欲望，並相互競爭。這樣的自由已經給世界帶來了巨大的混亂與災難。

什麼是自由？請你捫心自問。自由是可以選擇的嗎？你可以自由地選擇，可以自由地從此地走到彼地，接受各種不同的工作——如果不喜歡這一份工作，還可以去做另一份。你可以想自己所想，並自由地表達心中所想。在民主社會裡，這麼做或許沒問題。但在極權主義國家卻行不通，因爲那裡沒有自由。

　　那麼，什麼是自由？它真的存在嗎？「自由」一詞的根本義中包含著愛的意思，而愛是可以選擇的嗎？我們必須要找到真正的自由是什麼。

　　自由有很多種，譬如你有避開某種事物的自由，有免遭痛苦的自由、免于憂慮的自由。有沒有哪種自由不是爲了避開某種事物的？其實想要避開某事的自由只是一種心理的反應而已。這就好比一個囚犯在監獄裡說：「我必須離開監獄。」從心理上講，我們同樣是生活在監獄中，而當痛苦、醜陋和不滿到來時，就希望能夠避開這種痛苦、醜陋和不滿。因此，我們想要的這種自由與囚犯想要的自由實際上是一樣的。那麼，深刻、內在、真實而不可撼動的自由是什麼？能讓你避開某種事物的自由又是什麼？

　　讓我們一起來探討這些問題。任何人都希望能夠免於束縛。大多數人都非常孤獨，他們希望通過各種各樣的娛樂形式——不管是宗教的還是世俗的——來擺脫、逃避這種孤獨。但有沒有一種自由並非這種心理的反應？要想瞭解這一點，我們必須先知道什麼是愛。愛是一種反應嗎？是一種吸引嗎？不管是性方面的還是其他方面的吸引？請自問這些問題，並找出正確的答案。

　　你如何才能找到正確答案？當有問題提出，你自然會去回答。如果你一直在思考這個問題，即是對這個問題作出反應。隨後你對自己的反應作出反應，得出答案。所以說，找到答案的過程，實際上就是在對話，對話內容便是提問、回答，或者回答、提問。如果我們一直維持著這種答案─問題─問題─答案的模式，那麼在這個過程中，你消失了，作為演講者的我也消失了，剩下的便只有問題。而那個問題也就有了生命力。你可以自己檢驗一下這些話。這就好比是一朵玫瑰花蕾，如果你把問題放在空氣裡，放在合適的位置上，它就會像花蕾一樣慢慢綻放，最終展現本質。問題的內在蘊含了自身的生命力、能量和驅動力。你是在對話，而不僅是接受別人的言論。

　　不受束縛的自由是愛嗎？而愛是一種反應嗎？也許對於多數人來說，愛並不存在。請記住，我只是在問問題，並沒有說愛真的不存在。許多人可能並不知道愛是什麼。我們知道吸引，知道柔情、憐憫、罪惡、悔恨和妒忌。這些是愛嗎？如果不是，那愛就是沒有反應的。而這就是自由，並非來自於某種反應的自由。理解這點非常重要，它並非智慧上、口頭上的，而是對其內在美的深刻理解。

　　當我們談論生活的藝術時，也必須問一下什麼是美。偉大的建築、歐洲的大教堂以及世界各地的神廟和清真寺，傑出的建築師、畫家和雕塑家如米開朗基羅的作品，都是美。那麼，美是人造的嗎？請運用你的大腦去尋找答案。老虎並不是人造的，謝天謝地！生長在野外的一棵古樹，孤傲挺拔，自成一景，它也不是人造的。但你畫這棵樹的時候，它便是人造的了；你會讚美它，去博物館欣賞偉大藝術家為它畫的傑作。因此，生活藝術的另一部分就是去理解自由的深度、自由的美和自由的善。

生命中的美學品質源於敏感，源於行動中的所有感覺（不是某種特定的感覺）。顯然，美只有在自我不存在時才會存在。我不在，故美在。我不在，故愛在。

因此，愛、自由、美、善是一體不分離的。它們之間相互關聯。「善」是個非常古老的詞，它有著極為深刻的內涵，這種深度只有在存在自由、愛與美的時候才能被感覺到。

什麼是欲望？它的來源是什麼？它是怎樣產生的？欲望是否源於人所感知到的事物？例如我看到了一輛漂亮的小車，是這種視覺造成了欲望嗎？請大家注意，不要只是同意我說的話。我們現在是從反面來看，所以不要落入言語的陷阱。如果你看到了一座非常好看的房子，於是說：「天哪，我多麼希望擁有這座房子。」那麼可以由此認為，是事物創造了欲望嗎？

我們必須非常仔細地探究什麼是欲望，但並不是說要壓制它或屈服於它。我們必須一起探究，而不是讓他人告訴我們答案。當你看到一個物體、一輛車或一位美女，或看到公園裡的一棵婀娜多姿的樹時說：「啊，我多麼希望擁有這樣一座公園。」你瞭解這種欲望嗎？你看到某個事物，產生相應的視覺，又因為這視覺而生出另一種知覺。那麼，這種知覺又會產生什麼呢？觸覺是知覺的一部分。如果你此前聽說過這一點，就不要再重複回答了，因為那沒什麼意義。那麼，在形成視覺、觸覺、知覺之後，還會出現什麼呢？

　　去仔細地尋找答案吧。例如，我看到商店櫥窗裡有一款非常精美的手錶，於是走進店裡，檢查它、觸摸它、感覺它，推測它的重量，檢驗它的材質。那這之後會發生什麼事呢？之後思想就會介入，並創造一個影像，說：「我想擁有它。」也就是說，先是產生視覺、觸覺、知覺，然後思想迅速創造出想要擁有這塊表的影像，欲望誕生。

　　現在，你覺得視覺、觸覺、知覺之間存在間隔嗎？在思想具象化地創造某個影像之前，有間隔嗎？你看得到嗎？整個過程的進展是那麼迅速，但當你像欣賞慢鏡頭重播一樣去看，就會看清所有的一切。這就是欲望。讓我們把間隔進一步拉大。你就是欲望，你就是思想和欲望的結構。因此，如果你能夠理解，能夠深入思想的本質並觀察自己的反應，那麼你就可以讓整個過程慢下來，它會因而顯得非常平靜，讓你可以深入理解。當然，你還需要給予一定的注意力與激情去尋找答案。

　　理解了欲望的本質和結構，我們就可以發現冥想的實質。有意識的沉思是冥想嗎？顯然不是。如果我有意識地坐在這裡，早上花二十分鐘，中午花二十分鐘，晚上再花二十分鐘，這就只是一種放鬆，一種美好、舒適、愉悅的小憩。那麼，什麼是冥想呢？如果你有意識地去沉思，它就會帶有方向、動機或成功的欲望。這顯然不是冥想，不是嗎？這就好比是一名普通職員晉升為經理。晉升與沉思兩件事情實際上是一樣的：一個被稱為「事業」，另一個被稱為「宗教成就」，但其實質並無區別。那些冥想的人是否看到了這一點？當然沒有。認同這一點，就意味著他們放棄了自己的「小」快樂、「小」娛樂。

　　之所以說有意識的沉思不是冥想，是因為這種沉思源於欲望：我要取得什麼，我要成為什麼——即自我要成為什麼（這裡的自我，也就是「我」），例如要成為神。這聽起來或許十分愚蠢。請原諒我使用「愚蠢」這個詞。那麼，什麼是冥想呢？如果冥想不是有意識的沉思，又是什麼？

　　「冥想」不僅有沉思、思考的意思，而且還有揣度之意。揣度也是梵語中「冥想」一詞的根本義之一。現在，你的大腦能夠停止揣度嗎？我現在是這樣，希望變成那樣；我把自己和你進行比較：你是那麼漂亮、優雅，那麼有思想、有深度，你的衣服是那麼的有品位，而我則不是。這都是在揣度，在比較。你能夠停止比較嗎？不要急著點頭說是。試試看，停止比較，看看沒有比較的生活是怎樣的。

因此，冥想並不是一種有意識、有準備的行為。冥想其實與思想和欲望都毫無關聯。冥想時，人的大腦真正處於「空」的狀態，思想以及人類所創造的任何事物都不在其中，因而你也就擁有了足夠的空間。在這樣的空間裡，必然是靜謐和充滿能量的。但如果你整天都想著自己——實際上大多數人都是如此，就等於是把大腦的這種非凡能力集中運用到了自己的瑣事上。如此一來，你也就沒有了空間。

我並非大腦方面的專家，但我長期以來一直在做自我研究，並觀察他人。大腦有它自己獨立運作的規律，當大腦處於完全靜謐、安寧的狀態時，那就是不可言喻的永恆之境。

因此，愛並不是一種反應，因而它是自由的。哪里有愛，哪里就有智慧，這種智慧並非源於思想，它是獨立於大腦之外的。憐憫、愛、自由都是獨立於大腦之外的。因為大腦有局限性，它無法包容它們。

第十一章 | 冥想的祝福

這就是冥想：
去探尋觀察者（即你自己）的整個結構和本質。
觀察者即是被觀察者，
兩者都是你自身的一部分。
唯有冥想可以讓你認識到這種整體性和統一性。

生活是什麼？這並不是在問我們應該怎樣生活，也不是問生活的目的、意義、原則或者目標是什麼，而是在問，現在這樣的生活是什麼，日常的生活是什麼。因為這才是唯一的眞實，而其他所有的一切都是不眞實的，是虛假、虛幻的。

那麼，現在這種生活，我們的、個人的乃至全人類的生活，與人類創造的這個社會的關係是怎樣的呢？社會就像一座大監獄，我們就關在裡面。因此，我們即是社會，即是世界，世界與我們是密不可分的。

這裡所要探討的並不是抽象的東西，不是理想，而是眞實的存在，即我們的生活。我們的生活是什麼？如果注意觀察，你會發現自出生之日起至死亡時止的生活，就是永無休止的鬥爭，是永不停止的掙扎，是大喜、大悲、恐懼、絕望、孤獨、憎惡、厭煩、重複、單調的集合體。我們的生活，就是一份沉悶乏味的苦差事，或是了無生趣地在某間辦公室或工廠裡工作四十年，或是做一名家庭主婦，或是追求性快感，或是妒忌、嫉妒、挫敗，或是對成功的崇拜。只要認真觀察，你會發現讓我們備受折磨的日常生活便是如此。

但如果你只是追求各種形式的娛樂，無論是在教堂裡還是在足球場上，都只是為了娛樂，那就必然會遭遇其中的痛苦和問題。內心膚淺的人只是希望在教堂裡或足球場上得到解脫，並非真的對活動本身有興趣。生命是嚴肅的，嚴肅之中又包含了許多歡樂。而只有嚴肅對待生活的人才能夠解決生命存在的重大問題。

由此可見，日常的生活實際上是一份苦差事，沒有人可以否認這一點。只是我們並不知道該怎麼應對。既然我們希望找到一種不同的生活方式，那至少應該嘗試一下。在嘗試改變之前，要先理解生活「是什麼」，而非「應該是什麼」。我們必須先瞭解、觀察真實的生活。如果你只是想像，或只是在頭腦中設想如何改變它，那就無法進行真實的觀察，無法切實接觸到它。但只要認真去看，你就會發現改變的另一種特質──這正是我們現在所探討的。

首先要去看，實實在在地看，不要膽怯，不要勉強，不要帶著痛苦和抵抗情緒，你要切實地觀察此時此刻的生活。生活是一份苦差事，我們能否觀察它，能否與它同在，與它密切接觸並保持直接連結？現在問題出來了：想要與所觀察的事物保持直接連結，那麼在你與它之間必不可有任何影像存在。這種影像指的是語言、徵象，或是無數個昨日的記憶。譬如說，你與妻子或丈夫的關係即是基於影像的關係，而這種影像是建立在許多年的快樂、性愛、嘮叨、沉悶、重複以及支配的基礎之上。你有關於她的影像，她有關於你的影像，這兩種影像的接觸即是所謂的「關係」。但很顯然，這只是被我們認定爲是一種關係，其實並不是，你並沒有與對方保持直接的連結。

與現實、「實相」的直接接觸同樣不存在。觀察者與被觀察者之間是分裂的。這說法看起來很複雜，但只要安靜地傾聽，你會發現其實很簡單。這種分裂，或者說彼此之間的屏障，就是語言、記憶，是所有衝突發生的地方。也就是自我，即是「我」。「我」是一個累積的影像，是無數個往昔記憶與思想，因爲其中並不存在與「實相」的直接接觸。不管你是譴責「實相」，合理化「實相」，接受或是爲它辯護，那也都只是言語上的表現，其中並不存在實際的接觸。這樣一來，對「實相」的理解和決斷也就無從談起。

我會對此簡單解釋，希望你能夠明白。人們總是習慣於嫉妒，而嫉妒是一個量度，是一種比較。有的人聰明、有才能，頭上頂著成功的光環，備受讚譽，而另一個人，比如說「我」，則不具備這一切。通過這樣的比較與揣度，人的嫉妒心自孩提時代就養成了。當你看到某個事物，看到某個不屬於自己的東西時，便心生豔羨、嫉妒。但嫉妒即是觀察者，觀察者與被觀察者之間並無分裂。觀察者對嫉妒是無能爲力的，因爲他既是嫉妒的因，又是嫉妒的果。因此，「實相」，即我們的日常生活及它的所有問題、恐懼、嫉妒、妒忌、絕望、孤獨，與說「我很孤獨」的觀察者是沒有區別的。觀察者本身即是孤獨，是嫉妒、是恐懼。因而，觀察者對「實相」無能為力。這並不是說他就接受、滿足於「實相」。但當與「實相」不存在衝突（這種衝突源於觀察者與被觀察者之間的分裂）、不產生抵觸的時候，你就會看到徹底的轉變。

而這就是冥想：去探尋觀察者（即你自己）的整個結構和本質。觀察者即是被觀察者，兩者都是你自身的一部分。唯有冥想可以讓你認識到這種整體性和統一性，而在冥想中是沒有任何衝突的，因而一切分裂都已消融，你也就超越了「實相」。

然後，你應該問自己：愛是什麼？雖然「愛」這個詞已經被賦予了過多的含義，已經在政客、牧師以及各種雜誌的評說議論中遭到「污染」，但我們仍要一同探討這個問題。愛是什麼？這不是在問愛應當是什麼、理想中的愛是什麼、終極的愛是什麼，而是問我們所擁有的愛是什麼？在我們通常稱之為「愛」的事物中，其實包含著恨、妒忌和巨大的痛苦。我們並非憤世嫉俗，只是要觀察真正的「實相」，觀察我們稱之為愛的東西。愛是恨嗎？是妒忌嗎？是對妻子或丈夫的佔有與支配嗎？

人們總是說自己愛家人，愛孩子。那麼，你愛你的孩子嗎？如果你全心全意地愛孩子，而不是只表現在口頭上，那麼你覺得明天還會有戰爭嗎？如果你愛你的孩子，你會教育、培訓、強迫他們遵從和接受一個腐化社會的既定秩序嗎？如果你真的愛你的孩子，會允許他們在戰場上慘遭屠殺嗎？如果你正在做著這一切，那根本不是愛。愛不是柔情百轉，不是甜言蜜語。總而言之，愛並不是快樂。

我們必須要理解快樂，因為對我們來說，愛、性和快樂是交織在一起的。談到愛時，我們說的往往是性快感和心理上的快樂。請注意，這裡並沒有否認快樂。當看到夕陽下的翠色山巒、山火中餘生的參天大樹、被一場大雨沖刷殆盡的積塵以及天上閃爍的星辰時，那是一種快樂。但那並不是我們所要談論的快樂。我們要關注的是感觀知覺上的快樂，以及來源於智慧和情感等方面的快樂。

和恐懼一樣，快樂也是由思想造成的。假設你昨天曾經走進一座靜謐的峽谷，欣賞四方的壯麗美景。彼時彼刻，你會感受到一種莫大的快樂和喜悅。而現在想起時，思想就會介入其中，並說，要是能再去一次該多好啊！回想一下昨日的體驗，不管是欣賞婀娜的樹木、壯麗的天空還是雄偉的山巒，都是快樂；或者追憶昨夜春宵一刻，那也是快樂。思想會想起往日的快樂之事，一想到這些，那便是快樂的開始。而同樣的，你也會想明天可能發生的不快樂之事。比如說你可能失去工作，可能遭遇變故，健康狀況出問題，一想到這些，那便是痛苦、恐懼的開始。

所以說，思想既創造了恐懼，也創造了快樂。對我們來說，愛即是思想，因為愛對我們而言就是快樂，而快樂是思想孕育出來的產物。這種快樂不是實實在在地欣賞日落與享受性生活，而只是對過去的記憶。因此，我們所說的愛是由思想創造和孕育、維持和延續的。如果非常仔細地去觀察，你會發現這是一個顯而易見、無可否認的事實。

於是，你可能會問：愛真的是思想嗎？思想可以培育出愛嗎？或者，思想可以培育出快樂嗎？思想是可以培育快樂，但它無論如何也不能培育出愛；同樣，它無論如何也培育不出謙虛。因此，愛並不是快樂，不是欲望。但你不能否定欲望或快樂。當你觀察這個世界，看到美麗的樹或漂亮的面孔時，你會在那一刻產生莫大的快樂。但隨後思想就會介入，給予足夠的空間和時間，讓記憶和快樂不斷增長。當你意識到這一點，理解了與愛相關聯的快樂的結構和本質時（這種理解是冥想的一部分），你就會發現這種愛是完全不同的。如此一來，你就會真正愛你的孩子，真正創造一個嶄新的世界。當明白了什麼是愛，不管你做什麼事情，都不會有錯。只有在你像過去一樣追求快樂的時候，事情才會變得一團糟。

另外一個問題，就是死亡。我們已經探討了日常生活是什麼的問題，進行了一次心靈之旅，以尋求愛的答案。現在，讓我們再探討一下死亡意味著什麼。如果你瞭解死亡，就會理解這個極其重要的問題，死亡之後的事情對你而言也就不重要了。

死亡不可避免。就如同經常使用的機器一樣，任何有機體都會因衰老或疾病而不可避免地走向生命的盡頭。對我們來說，衰老是一件恐怖的事情。你可曾注意到秋日的落葉，它那麼優雅、柔和、漂亮，卻又是那麼的脆弱，那麼的不堪一擊。而我們隨著年齡的增長，將會看到自己的虛偽、缺陷、醜陋。衰老之所以令人恐懼，是因爲我們在青年時代、中年時代都不曾正確地生活。我們一直處於恐懼之中，害怕生存，害怕死亡，從未眞正地生活過。而隨著年齡的增長，所有那些事情都在我們身上發生了。

因此，我們要找出死亡的含義是什麼，要知道所有的生命最終都會走向死亡，而人在面臨死亡之時，必然會在某種死而復生或輪回轉世的理論中尋求希望和安慰。亞洲人習慣於接受輪回轉世的理論，他們對此作了大量的探討和論述，並將自己的整個生命都寄託于來世。但他們忘記了最重要的一個問題：如果還有來生，那麼你今生就必須正確地生活。因而，這也就意味著你的來生與你此生所做之事有著莫大的關係，包括如何生活、做了什麼、想了什麼、說了什麼以及你的思想是如何運轉的。如果你現在沒有正確地生活，那麼來生就會得到這種不正確生活的「獎賞」，即懲罰。但他們把這一切都忘了，而只是談論輪回轉世的美好，談論公平的美好，談論各種雞毛蒜皮的瑣事。

其實，雖然不能通過某種理論逃避現實，但卻可以無畏地面對現實。既然生命最終會走向死亡，那麼從心理層面、從內在角度來看，死亡意味著什麼？在死亡即將來臨之時，你是沒有任何爭辯餘地的，你不能說：「求你了，再多給我幾天時間吧，我還沒有寫完我的書，還沒有成爲某個機構的首席執行長，還沒有成爲大主教，再等一會兒吧。」你是不能爭辯的。因此，人必須從內在、從心理上理解死亡。死亡是過去所有一切的終結，包括你所有的快樂，珍藏的所有記憶，擁有的一切物品。死亡在日復一日地持續，這並非理論上的說法，而是實實在在的眞相。例如昨日的快樂昨日就會死亡，不會再延續到今日。只有這樣活著，我們的大腦才能夠永葆清新、年輕、單純和敏感，才能夠進入冥想狀態。

如果你已經清楚美德的基礎，即關係中的秩序，那麼你就能明白愛與死亡的特質，即它們就是生活的全部。於是，你的大腦會變得異常安寧、平靜，這種靜是發自內心的、自然的，並非通過強制性的紀律、控制或壓制而得到。這種靜意涵深遠，除此之外沒有其他任何語言或描述可以形容它。這樣一來，大腦就不會再去探究思想的絕對眞理，因爲已經毫無必要。原因就在於，靜默中存有眞正的實相。

而這一切就是冥想的祝福。

第十二章 | 偉大的生命

在人的生命中，
聲音有著非常重要的意義。
例如大海的聲音，
妻子或丈夫的聲音，
還有風吹樹葉、大海揚波的聲音，
以及樹木的靜謐之聲，
皆有豐富的內涵。

生命中有傾聽的藝術、學習的藝術、感知的藝術。傾聽的藝術並不僅僅是聽別人說。二者是截然不同的。傾聽意味著你是真正地在聽，沒有解讀，沒有同意與否，沒有抵觸情緒，只是在聽，不帶有自己的結論、偏見、看法、判斷。這需要一定的注意力，而在這種注意力中，作為傾聽者的你已經不存在了，只剩下純粹的聽。當我們集中注意力去聽的時候，就不會再有同意與否的表示，我們只是處於注意力高度集中的狀態。

你不僅在傾聽演講者所講的話時要這樣，在聽妻子或丈夫說話時也要如此，而後者相對要更難一些，因為你們已經熟悉彼此。幸運的是，此刻你並不瞭解正在演講的我，我也不瞭解你，所以你可以不帶任何偏見地去傾聽我演講。這也意味著你需要高度的敏感來喚醒你的感覺，以便全身心地投入到傾聽之中。

如果一個人能夠如此聚精會神地傾聽，奇跡就會發生。這並不是要你去傾聽觀點與觀點之間的辯論，或者論斷與論斷之間的交鋒

——不論那些論斷有多合理或多荒謬，而是要學會在靜默之中傾聽。

這樣的傾聽是自然的，你不僅僅要用耳朵去聽，還要用上所有的感覺去聽。此時，你就不存在了，只剩下聲音。在人的生命中，聲音有著非常重要的意義。例如大海的聲音，妻子或丈夫的聲音，還有風吹樹葉、大海揚波的聲音，以及樹木的靜謐之聲，皆有豐富的內涵。

這就是傾聽的藝術。至於學習的藝術，它並非記憶的積累。人在學校裡學習數學、生物、物理等，形成相關的記憶，成為見識廣博之人。人的大腦廣泛收集資訊，存儲數學、地理或歷史知識——只要是喜歡的就都存儲起來，並將它們用以謀生，而不理會對這些知識的運用是否熟練。因此，知識是靜態的。你可以增加也可以減少它的存儲，但它在本質上就是靜態而非動態的。動態的事物無法增加或減少，而知識不是。知識只是資訊的積累、經驗的存儲。那些保存起來的知識並非動態的，像河水般流動的事物才是動態的。

如果你想成為一名工程師、飛行員或物理學家，就必須積累知識。這是必要的，但增加的那部分其實是已知的，知識就這樣逐漸轉變為靜態。而相應的，是你在學習過程中一直在運動，從未停留在同一處。學習就是當下對知識的運用，及對其正確與否的檢驗。如果是正確的，那就付諸行動吧。

畢竟，在這個世界上，理論和實踐（或者說是生命）之間毫無關聯。人們總有滿肚子的理論和各種各樣的可能性，實踐起來卻是另一回事。因此有必要學習，它是一個整體的運動，而非像知識一樣是片段化的。學習就如奔騰的江河，時時刻刻都處於運動之中。

再說說感知的藝術。感知與看不同。感知並不涉及時間，而看以及將所看之物轉化為行動目標則與時間相關。例如我看到了自己應該去做什麼，然後再去做這件事，；在看和做之間存在一個間隙或者間隔，這個間隙就是時間。你看到了應該做的事情，然後考慮、思索、探究，看看是否可以做、是否有利可圖……所有的這一切都意味著行動之前存在時間間隔。

與之相對應地，感知既是看也是做，因而行動和感知之間並不存在間隔。例如，我看到、覺察到自己不應該成為一名印度教徒，因為人們成為印度教徒多半是為了尋求安全庇護，而這也是造成戰爭的原因之一。民族主義、宗族主義都是戰爭的肇因。

我看到了這一點，感到這是正確的，所以我不再是一名印度教徒。同樣，如果你看到了成為一名伊斯蘭教徒、印度教徒、佛教徒或基督教徒的危險性，你就會迅速行動起來──你的反應會像看到了眼鏡蛇那樣迅速。

以上就是傾聽、學習和感知的藝術。如果能夠與此等藝術同在，那麼你的生命將會是非凡的。這就需要高度的敏感、關愛和注意力。

第十三章 ｜ 死亡的藝術

你不能帶走金錢、家人、知識、信仰。
死亡說你必須將這些留在身後。
你同意嗎？或者，你會拒絕？
要面對這個問題，不要回避。

和你一樣，多數人都懼怕死亡。死亡是人的基本恐懼之一。包括你我在內的每一個人，最終都無法逃脫死亡，都會死去。這是不容置疑的。也許你會比他人活得久一些，而且過著簡單、健全、理性的生活，沒有虛耗光陰。但不管你採用何種生活方式，都難免一死。這是事實。

你會面對現實嗎？你會死，我也會。這裡說到「你」，那麼「你」是誰？女士們、先生們，你是誰？你有錢，有地位，有實力，你不誠實，你的困惑、憂慮和孤獨，你的銀行帳戶，所有這一切不就是你嗎？簡單一點，誠實一點吧。這就是你。而我們要問的是，在面臨死亡的時候，該掌握怎樣的生活的藝術？什麼樣的生活藝術可以讓人不再懼怕死亡？

讓我們一同來探討，不是從智慧上或理論上，而是去做真正的探討，以便幫助你理解死亡。我們並不提倡自殺。有一些哲學家、存在主義者表示，生命就是永不停止地上坡、下坡——當你到達一定的高度後，便開始走下坡路。他們認爲這種生命毫無意義，因而也就提倡自殺。但我們並不認同。自殺不是生活的藝術。我們要問自己爲什麼懼怕死亡。爲什麼無論青年還是老人，都會爲此擔驚受怕、深感恐懼？這種恐懼可能是有意識的，也可能是無意識的。而害怕死亡也意味著害怕苦難——害怕遭受與家人訣別的苦難、與所擁有的一切事物分離的苦難。

因此，生活的藝術並不僅僅是找出日常的生存之道，而且還意味著要找出死亡的意義所在。

什麼是死亡？生物學上的死亡，是有機體的死亡，比如說因爲疾病、衰老、事故或某種災難而死。死亡對我們來說意味著什麼？如果你理解了，那麼對你而言，死亡將不再僅僅是有機體的壽命終結，你將能接受生與死總是相依相隨的現實。

思考一下這個問題。問問你自己，看能否掌握這種生活的藝術，接納死亡。要想找到答案，你必須知道什麼是生存，生存和死亡哪個更重要。大多數人都看重後者，寄希望於輪回轉世之類的理論，但卻從未思考過生存，而生存比死亡更重要，那是一種藝術。人如果過著正確的生活，那麼死亡也是這正確生活的一部分，而不是意味著愚蠢生命的終結。

那麼，什麼是生存？我們可以就此進行討論與對話，但你必須自己來回答這個問題。你的生命是怎樣的？你的日常生活是怎樣的？你的生命實際上就是長期以來的一系列日常生活的集合，我們的日常生活中總是充滿痛苦、憂慮、不安全感、不確定性、對於某些事物的假想、某些虛幻而不真實的存在、虛假的生命以及信念、信仰。這就是你。你依戀你的房子、金錢、銀行帳戶，依戀妻子和孩子。因此你是被束縛的，這就是你的生命。你一直都在掙扎，生活裡充滿了努力、不快、痛苦、孤獨、悲傷。你的生命便是如此。你懼怕失去所擁有的一切。而死亡說：「我的朋友，你不能把這些帶走。」你不能帶走你的金錢、家人、知識、信仰。死亡說你必須將這些留在身後。你同意嗎？或者，你會拒絕？要面對這個問題，不要回避。

死亡對你說：「當我到來時，你必須放棄這一切。」現在，你可能放棄這一切嗎？你會放棄嗎？你依戀自己的傢俱，你必須擦洗它、保養它，而不會放棄它，它是你的，它就是你的一部分。當你依戀某件傢俱時，那件傢俱就是你。可是死亡會說：「我的朋友，你不能帶走那張桌子。」那麼，你能否完全放棄對那件傢俱的依戀？這就是死亡。所以，生與死是相依相隨的，它們每時每刻都陪伴著你。

你可以看到死亡的美，看到它給予你的自由、能量和能力。當你存有依戀的時候，就會產生恐懼、憂慮、不確定性，而不確定性、恐懼會導致悲傷。悲傷是生命的一部分。地球上的任何一個人都會遭受苦難，都會流淚。你有沒有流過淚？如果丈夫不關心你，你們彼此利用，而當你突然意識到這一切是多麼醜陋時，就會感到痛苦。在歷史長河中，人類以宗教的名義、以神的名義、以民族的名義殺戮不休，亦因此遭受了巨大的災難。而他們從來不曾將苦難終結。

有苦難的地方，就沒有愛存在。苦難中不僅包含有自憐，而且還有對孤獨、分離與分裂的恐懼。還有懊悔與罪惡，全都包含在「苦難」這個詞中。我們從來都沒有解決過這一問題，就這樣忍受、流淚，帶著對兒子、兄弟、妻子或丈夫的回憶度過餘生。這樣的悲傷有盡頭嗎？或者，我們必須永遠背負著悲傷？找出這個問題的答案，沒有恐懼、沒有悲傷地活著，同樣是生活的藝術。

生命的疑問之一，就是我們有沒有可能過一種沒有悲傷的生活。什麼是悲傷？兒子的去世會令你悲傷，尤其如果你是一位母親的話。所謂一朝懷胎，十月分娩，你生他、養他、看護他、照顧他。這其中包含了一位母親的痛苦、快樂和幸福，而最終他卻死了。為了你的國家，他被殺死了。你為什麼允許這種事情發生？

什麼是悲傷？悲傷是你的兒子去世，再也不能回來了嗎？雖然你認為你們還將在來生相見，但他已經離去了。這是事實。但你一直保留著對兒子的記憶和他的照片。你生活在這種記憶中，終日以淚洗面、無法忘卻。這成爲你心頭的一個負擔。此外，你們卻從未探究過悲傷與苦難，從未問過這種悲傷和苦難是否會結束。不是問它們會否在人生命終止的時候結束，而是要問會否在當下、在今日結束。

你是因爲自憐而悲傷嗎？是因爲你年輕的兒子死了嗎？是因爲他鮮活的生命不在了嗎？是因爲你依戀他嗎？不要逃避回答。這種依戀是怎樣的？你在依戀誰？你的兒子嗎？「你的兒子」對你來說意味著什麼？要保持理性和邏輯。你的兒子是什麼？你有一張他的照片，上面有他的影像，你希望他成爲一個優秀的人。他是你的兒子，而你之所以對他如此依戀，是因爲他將接管你的生意，賺得更多的錢。

此外，你還對他傾注了一份情感——它還不能稱爲愛，而只能說是一種特殊的情感。如果你眞的愛你的兒子，那就會採取另外一種不同的教育方式與撫養方式，而不僅僅是讓他追隨你的人生步伐。他是新的一代，與你這一代可能完全不同。也許你希望他成爲新的一代，成爲一個與你不一樣的人。你還希望他繼承你的財產、房子。可是隨著他的死亡，這一切都幻滅了。多麼殘酷。這正是造成巨大悲傷的原因之一。

而死亡，理所當然地會帶來最後一刻的悲傷。但如果你已了脫生死，那麼一切都不會有變化。對你來說，每天都是新生——誕生出全新的「你」。而在這個全新的「你」當中，有著無與倫比的美。這就是創造，其中便包含著莫大的自由。「自由」一詞的根本義就是愛。由此可見，生活和死亡的藝術二者相結合，帶來了偉大的愛。愛有它自己的智慧，它並非來自詭異的大腦的智慧，而是獨立於大腦之外的。

第十四章 | 觀察是唯一的真理

真正的觀察不僅要目不轉睛、聚精會神，
而且還要運用你的內心與頭腦。
如果你只是用了內在智性的一小部分去生活、
工作、思考與行動，
那就不可能完全看清所觀察的事物。

觀察是非常重要的。它要求觀察者必須高度集中注意力去觀察，是一門很高的藝術。我們的觀察通常非常片面，從未用上全部的智慧與心思，去對某個事物進行透徹的觀察。我想，除非已經掌握了這門偉大的藝術，否則，我們就只是運用了心智與大腦的一部分去行動與生活。

我們從未透徹觀察過任何一個事物，這是因爲我們過多關注自己的問題，或是受到了信仰、傳統與過往的太多束縛，這就阻礙了我們去觀察或傾聽。我們從未用心看過一棵樹，只是通過自己擁有的對樹的影像與概念去觀察。而這種概念、知識與經驗，和眞實的樹截然不同。在看一棵樹的時候，你會發現要想對它進行透徹觀察是多麼困難。但唯有這樣，你的所見與實相之間才不會存在影像或屏障的隔閡。這裡所說的透徹是指用上你全部的智慧和心思，而不是只用其中的一部分。我們的觀察要麼是情緒化的、感情用事的，要麼就是十分理智的，這明顯阻礙了我們對色彩、光之美、樹木與鳥兒的真實觀察。我們從未與它們有過直接聯結。

　　我十分懷疑我們是否真的與所觀察的事物有過聯結，哪怕觀察的是自己的信念、思想、動機、感想。即使是在觀察自己時，我們的觀察中也總是有影像存在。

　　觀察是唯一的真理，理解這一點很重要，除此之外，別無他法。如果我知道如何去觀察一棵樹、一隻鳥、一張可愛的面孔或一個孩子的笑容，那麼所見即是實相，沒有必要再去做其他的任何事情以探尋真相。但這種對鳥、樹葉的觀察，以及對鳥鳴聲的傾聽，卻已成為幾乎不可能做到的事情，因為我們早前已經建立了一種有關大自然與他人的影像。這實際上阻礙了我們去真實地觀察和感受，而這種感受與情感和情緒是截然不同的。

　　正如前面所說，我們對事物的觀察都是片面的。自孩提時代起，我們便養成了片面觀察、片面學習、片面生活的習慣。在我們心中，還有一片異常廣闊的區域是自己從未觸及或從不知道的。我們的心有著廣闊的、不可測的空間，但我們卻從未觸及它。我們從未運用全部的心智、心思、神經、眼睛乃至耳朵，去透徹地觀察任何一個事物，所以並不瞭解那個空間的特質。對我們來說，最重要的是語言、概念，而非所見與所為。但這種概念化的生活方式，也就是帶著某種概念（比如信仰、理想）去生活，卻阻礙了實際的觀察和行動。因而我們面臨著行動的問題，面臨著什麼該做、什麼不該做的問題。這樣一來，行動和概念之間就產生了衝突。

請觀察我正在談論的事，而不僅僅是聽我的演講，你要自己去觀察，並將演講者當作一面鏡子，這樣你就會看到自己的影子。演講者講的話並不重要，演講者本人也不重要，你對自己的觀察才是重要的。我們的內在心靈、生活方式、個人感受與日常活動必須經歷一場徹底的革命與全面的改變，而只有當你知道如何觀察的時候，如此根本、深刻的革命才有可能發生。

真正的觀察不僅要目不轉睛、聚精會神地「觀察」，而且還要運用你的內心與頭腦。如果你只是用了內在智性的一小部分去生活、工作、思考與行動，那就不可能完全看清所觀察的事物。

看看這個世界上正在發生什麼。我們正受到所處社會與文化的束縛，而這種文化正是人類製造的產物。文化不是神聖的，不是天賜的，亦非永恆的。文化、社會、書籍、廣播，我們聽著、看著，有意識或無意識地接受它們的影響，這一切都慫恿我們生活在頭腦的廣闊空間中的一個極小角落裡。從小學到大學，你最終學到了一種謀生技能；而在接下來的四五十年間，你的生命、時間、精力與思想，都會被局限在這個狹小的角落裡。頭腦有著廣闊的空間，除非我們在這種片段化的生活中進行一場激進的變革，否則根本不可能發生徹底的革命。雖然會有經濟上、社會上和所謂文化上的改變，但人類仍將遭受苦難，仍將處在衝突、戰亂、痛苦、悲傷和絕望之中。

你可以成為一名優秀的律師、一流的工程師、藝術家或偉大的科學家，但這只是整體生命中的一個片段。你應該真實地去觀察當下正在發生的事情。共產主義者、資本主義者、父母、學校官員、教育者們都一直在調適他們的頭腦，以使它能夠在某種模式與片段中發揮作用。人們所關心的，只是局限於這種模式與片段中的改變。

我們怎樣才能意識到這一點——不是從理論上或思想上，而是真正看到實際現狀？所謂實際現狀就是每天正在發生的事，是報紙的報導、政客的口號，是文化和傳統、家中的話語。在觀察時，如果真的看到了這些破碎的現實片段，那麼你就會問：「如何才能讓頭腦完全行動起來？」你必須這樣問自己，我想你也一定會問。當然，我所說的頭腦並不是片段化的、受限的，亦非受過教育、有智慧的頭腦，更不是恐懼的、總想著「神在這裡」或「神不在這裡」或者「這是我的家庭、你的家庭、我的國家、你的國家」的頭腦。

然後，你會問頭腦如何才能夠完全運轉起來，即便只是在學習一種技能時。你知道自己必須要學習一種技能，學習如何與人相處，如何在當今這個無序的社會裡生存。由此，你一定會問一個最根本的問題：「我們的整個頭腦如何才能變得足夠敏銳，以至於其中的任何一個部分都是敏感的？」

當前，我們並不敏感，頭腦中有一小塊區域是敏感的，當我們特有的個性、習慣或快樂遭到否定時，衝突就會產生。我們的頭腦只是在某個片段中、某個區域內具有敏感性，並非整個都是敏感的。那麼問題就來了：整體之中已經變得遲鈍的某個部分，如何才能夠變得像整體一樣敏感？

你可能從來都沒有問過自己這個問題，因為所有人都已經習慣了生活在那個狹小的角落裡，希望生活中的問題和衝突盡可能減少。我們欣賞這個小區域內的文化，並反對其他的文化，甚至不明白局促地生活在一個廣闊區域的角落裡意味著什麼。我們並不知道自己已經被深深地困在了那個角落，還一直試圖在那裡尋找問題的答案，因為我們關心的只是那個小角落。那麼，怎樣才能夠完全瞭解整個真相，開始敏感起來呢？

沒有任何方法。因為所有的方法、體系、重複或習慣都是局限在小角落裡的，而那個小角落只是廣闊的生命區域的一部分。我們首先要做的就是觀察那個角落的實際存在及其需求，然後再嘗試讓整個頭腦都變得完全敏感起來，這就是唯一而真正的變革。隨後，我們的行動就會發生變化，思想、感受也會徹底改變。但我沒有方法可以提供。不要問「我怎樣才能夠變得敏感」之類的問題。上大學、讀書或按照別人說的去做，都不會讓你變得敏感。因為這一切都已經是局限在那個小角落裡的，只會讓你越來越不敏感，甚至麻木不仁、殘忍、狂暴。這樣的事例在日常生活中都可以見到。而我們之所以麻木，是因為自己只是在一個無序世界中的小角落裡運轉、生活和行動。

沒有任何方法。請務必明白這一點，這樣就不用再屈服于那些權威的巨大壓力之下，因而也就擺脫了過去的束縛。顯然，這個過去指的就是社會文化中的傳統、信仰、記憶，等等。在我們看來，它們是如此的美妙。而當你意識到沒有任何方法可以擺脫那個「小角落」時，就能夠將過去的一切永遠放下，不再受其束縛。但你還是必須瞭解那個小小的角落，以擺脫使自己變得遲鈍的負擔。

那麼，既然沒有方法，現在我們應該做什麼？方法意味著實踐，意味著依賴，依賴於你的或我的方法，依賴於這個人或那個人的路線。你可以翻閱現代心理學家或古代導師的相關論著，通過書本來尋找答案。但不要相信他們的話，因為你要自己去找答案，而不是依靠別人。關鍵就在於我們並不瞭解心的深度和廣度，並不瞭解心靈，所以不可能形成任何關於它的想法、看法或知識。這樣一來，我們就擺脫了所有假想和神學的束縛。

既然如此，那我們該做什麼呢？你所要做的就是去觀察。觀察廣闊區域中的那個角落，觀察你在角落裡建造的小房子，那是你生活、奮鬥、爭吵、成長的地方。你瞭解那裡發生的所有事情。去觀察吧！

理解觀察的意義之所以非常重要，是因為你所處的那個孤立的角落裡存在著衝突。有觀察的地方就不會有衝突。這也正是為什麼人必須從頭開始——不，不是從頭開始，而是從現在開始——學習觀察的原因。從現在開始，而不是從明天開始，因為「明天」並不存在。所謂「明天」，只是源於對快樂、恐懼或痛苦的探尋。從心理上講，其實並不存在明天，但我們的大腦、我們的心發明了時間。

你必須做的事情就是去觀察。如果你不敏感，就無法觀察；而如果在你和被觀察者之間存在影像，那你就不可能敏感。觀察是愛的行動。你知道是什麼讓人的整個頭腦都具有敏感性嗎？唯有愛。你可以學習技術，以及如何去愛；但如果只有技術卻沒有愛，那你就只會給這個世界帶來破壞。自己去觀察吧，用你的心智和心思去探索，就能看得到。

看、觀察和傾聽都是最偉大的行動。如果你只是站在小角落裡看問題，那就不可能看到這個世界上正在發生的事——絕望，憂慮，痛苦，孤獨，母親、妻子、情人以及那些被殺者的眼淚。你必須親眼看到這所有的一切，不要只是出於個人情緒或情感而說「我反對戰爭」或「我支持戰爭」，因為情感和情緒是最具破壞力的。它們避開了事實，因而也就避開了「真相」。

因此，觀察是至關重要的。觀察即是理解。你不可能通過心智、智慧或某個片段來理解。只有當心處於完全平和靜謐的狀態，即不存在任何影像時，才會有理解。

觀察將會打破所有的隔閡。只要你與樹木之間、與我之間、與鄰居之間——不論彼此相距千里還是只有一牆之隔——還存在著分離，那麼就一定會有衝突。分離意味著衝突，這道理顯而易見。我們生活在衝突中，而且已經習慣了衝突和分離。印度視自己為一個地理、政治、經濟、社會和文化單位，歐洲、美國、俄羅斯也是如此。它們都把自己看做一個相互分離、彼此獨立的單位，而這種分離註定要引發戰爭。這並不是說我們一定要達成共識，或是存在分歧時一定會有戰爭。當你真實地去觀察一個事物時，根本不存在同意不同意的問題。只有當你戴著有色眼鏡、帶著一己之見去觀察時，才會出現分歧和分離。

在觀察一棵樹的時候，如果你是真正地去看它，那麼你和樹之間就不會有分裂，觀察者已經不存在了。你不妨自己去觀察一棵樹、一朵花或是一個人的面龐，會發現你與它們之間並不存在距離。而只有當「愛」存在時，你才會有這樣的體驗。但在時下，「愛」這個詞已經被我們過度濫用了。真實的觀察可以消除時間和空間的隔閡；有了愛，時間和空間才會消失。你不可能擁有愛卻看不到美的存在。你可以談論美、描述美、設計美，但如果沒有愛，那麼就沒有什麼是美的。沒有愛意味著你並不夠敏感，以致不斷衰退。之所以如此，原因就在於你對整個人生都不敏感。

我們的基本問題並不在於如何阻止戰爭，或爭論哪個「神」更好，哪種政治體系或經濟體系更好，哪個政黨值得我們投票。不管你是生活在美國、印度、俄羅斯還是世界其他地區，所面臨的最基本問題就是如何擺脫「小角落」的束縛。而這個小角落其實就是我們自己，就是我們不誠實的心。我們之所以打造出這個小角落，是因為自己的頭腦已經被片段化了，因而也就失去了對整體的敏感性。從根本上講，每個人都追求快樂，自然希望這個角落可以給自己帶來安全、和平、安寧、滿足和快樂，讓自己擺脫所有痛苦。但如果你研究過自己的快樂，觀察、探究過它，你就會發現，哪里有快樂，哪里就有痛苦。二者密不可分，你不可能只有快樂沒有痛苦，或只有痛苦沒有快樂；而我們一直都希望有更多的快樂，因而也就產生了更多的痛苦。正是基於這樣的緣由，人們建立了自己稱為「人生」的小角落。觀察與生命是緊密相連的，如果你固守著自己的概念、信仰、信條或看法，那就不可能與生命保持密切的聯結。

因此，最重要的事情是觀察和傾聽。傾聽鳥的鳴叫聲，傾聽妻子的聲音，還有你自己的聲音，不管它有多麼刺耳、柔美或難聽。你會發現觀察者與被觀察者之間的所有分裂都不存在了，因而衝突也就消失了。由於你的觀察是如此的認真，以至於這種觀察成了一種紀律。而如果你能夠意識到的話，那麼這就是美，就是觀察之美。如果懂得觀察，你就不用再做其他的事情了，因為所有的紀律和美德，都包含在這觀察之中了，這樣的觀察，就是專注。

這種觀察中充滿了美，因而就有愛存在。於是，你也沒有什麼事情要做了。立身之處就是天堂，一切追求都將終結。

第十五章 | 自由自在的生命

人能否過上一種沒有任何衝突、
勞苦、束縛的生活？
我們總是在努力和掙扎，
生活中總有各種變化與變動，
因此充滿了掙扎、對抗和矛盾。

冥想在日常生活中處於何種地位？或者，冥想是獨立於我們的日常生活之外的？你是否認為一定要冥想，就像要做某件非做不可的事情一樣？你有沒有得出過這樣的結論，並將它帶入到生活中？或者，你有沒有試著找出自己的行為與整個意識覺醒之間的關係？

為什麼需要冥想？我們過著不快樂的、不堪重負的生活，其中充滿了衝突、不幸、苦難、欺騙。為什麼要把冥想引入到這樣的日常生活中？還是說，對內涵、結構、反應、衝突、悲傷、傲慢、自豪等等的理解都算是在冥想？

所謂把冥想引入生活中，並不是說你要先冥想，然後再把它付諸日常行為，而是指，當你去辦公室上班、在工廠工作、在農田耕作或是同你的妻子（丈夫）、兒女交流時，你知道自己的內在反應。在探究和理解這些反應，瞭解自己為什麼會感到嫉妒、為什麼會憂慮、會接受權威、會產生依賴時，這種探索本身就是冥想。這個順序如果反過來，就不是冥想。如果你先去冥想，然後再把自己所認為的這種冥想引入到日常生活與行動中，那麼就會產生衝突和矛盾。相反的，如果一個心懷嫉妒的人——我們大多數人都是如此——不是僅僅口頭上說說嫉妒是對是錯，或該不該產生嫉妒心，而是能夠真正看到嫉妒的本質，去探究並理解人們為什麼會嫉妒，進而去除這種心理，那麼這就是冥想。在這種冥想中沒有任何的衝突，而你要不斷去探索。你需要專心致志、非常認真地對待這件事，不是僅僅玩文字遊戲。

因此，當你開始探尋自己的存在（包括你的反應、你的意識狀態、為什麼你會相信、為什麼你不會相信、為什麼你會受制度的影響，等等）的整個本質和結構時，冥想就已經在你的日常生活中佔有一席之地了。你的存在即是冥想的實際運動。如果你能夠真正去探索，不僅僅停留在理論上，不是按照佛洛德或別的什麼心理學家、宗教導師的理論去理解，那麼你就能掌握意識的本質。你要探索自己的整個存在，即你的意識。

你可曾探尋過思想、思考的整個運動過程？思想、思考能看到它們自己在運動嗎？這是個非常重要的問題，如果你真的想要探尋，一定要先理解它。我可以說，通過信仰、恐懼、快樂、悲傷，「我已經察覺到自己的意識。」我能瞭解意識的內容，我會說，「是的，我害怕、貪婪、正在遭受痛苦，而且為人傲慢、充滿自豪。」這就是我所瞭解的意識的內容。通過這種方式，「我」便和

「我」的意識分開了。

這樣一來，「我」便是作爲觀察者，在觀察自己的意識。但這個「我」是貪婪、憂慮、恐懼、不安的，充滿了不確定性與悲傷感，而這些也就是「我」的意識，因此「我」和「我」的想法並沒有什麼不同。「我」和「我」的經歷、「我」的憂慮、恐懼等等並沒有什麼不同。「我」就是這一切。「我」或許認爲自己是神，但這種想法只是「我」的一部分，是「我」創造了神。

所以，觀察者就是被觀察者，也就是意識，那麼，這種意識能否覺察到它自身的運動？具體地說，憤怒本身能否覺察到憤怒的產生，而不存在一個憤怒的「我」？讓我們一起來探尋。人在憤怒的那一瞬間，還沒有產生對憤怒的認知。你有沒有注意到這一點？憤怒實際上只是一種狀態。在此之後，你才把它稱爲「憤怒」。這意味著你已經根據過去的經驗意識到了現在的狀態，意識到了當前正在發生的事，然後才說：「那是憤怒。」在憤怒的那一瞬間，你對這種反應是沒有認知的，也不會給它命名。但在這瞬間過去之後，它便有了名字。這種命名是源於過去的，是以過去的認知來看待當前的行動。那麼，你可以不命名，而只是去觀察嗎？在你命名的那一刻，你已經是在依據對它的認知強化了自己的反應。這是一個非常有趣的問題。

總而言之，文字並非事物。「帳篷」這個詞並不等於實實在在的帳篷，但對我們造成影響的卻是這個詞，而非事物本身。因此，理解並真正認識到「文字並非事物」這一事實就非常重要了。當憤怒出現的時候，不去命名它而只是去觀察，憤怒就會作為一種反應，漸漸消退。但在你命名的那一刻，便已經是在依據過去的認知將它強化了。

如果你已經明白了這個問題，那麼我們再討論下一個問題：感覺有無可能覺察到感覺本身？這並不是在問你能否覺察到感覺。現在我們的感覺都是分開的，分成了視覺、味覺、聽覺、嗅覺等等不同的部分。不過，是否存在將所有感覺都合而為一的整體運動呢？這個問題很有趣，因為我們將由此瞭解到，自己能否運用所用的感覺去觀察大海、高山、小鳥乃至你的親朋與至交。如果能的話，屆時你的觀察也就不再有中心。

請按照我說的去嘗試一下。不要立刻同意我所說的。親自去嘗試一下。當你聞到一股清香（例如雨後清晨、彌漫在空氣中的醉人氣息）時，一種特定的感覺就會被喚醒。但你能否用自己所有的感覺去感受清晨的這種清新與澄淨？

你要覺察自己的感官反應，不論只是其中某一種感官在反應，還是所有的感官都有反應。如果你只覺察到一種感覺，那是什麼感覺？如果只有鼻子對氣味的反應，那麼其他的感覺就會或多或少地處於擱置狀態。試試看，會發生什麼情況？我要問的是，當你在聞一朵花時，會不會出現所有感官的整體反應，也就是說，並不僅僅涉及嗅覺，而且還包括整個有機體的全部感覺？

當你聽到噪音時，能不能調動起所有的感覺，將自己融入噪音中，從而不致對它產生抵觸情緒或感到厭煩？在看起伏的山巒時——你或許每天傍晚和清晨都會眺望它——除了用眼睛（即視覺）之外，你能不能運用全部的感覺去看？如果能的話，那麼你的觀察也就不再有中心。試試看。用所有的感官去觀察，用所有的感覺去覺察。你會發現，自己第一次不是用遲鈍的眼睛和記憶去觀察一個事物。

於是問題又來了：思想能夠覺察到它本身嗎？你現在正在思考，對嗎？當我問你問題的時候，思考的整個運動就開始了。對嗎？顯然是這樣。那麼，這種思考本身能夠看到它自己在思考嗎？顯然不可能。

其實，我要問的是，人能否過上一種沒有任何衝突、勞苦、束縛的生活？我們總是在努力、在掙扎，生活中總有各種變化與變動，因此生命中充滿了掙扎、鬥爭和矛盾——「我必須做這件事，絕不能做那件事；我必須控制自己；我為什麼要控制自己？這種想法早已經過時了，我應該做自己想做的事。」所有這一切都是強制性的運動。我們能不能過上一種自由自在、沒有任何束縛的生活？但沒有束縛並不意味著你可以為所欲為。那種想法太幼稚了，因為我們根本就不可能為所欲為。哪里有控制，哪里就有衝突，就有鬥爭，而衝突和鬥爭也有諸多不同的表現形式，如暴力、壓制、神經質、寬容，等等。

因此，我問我自己，也問大家——我們能否過上沒有任何束縛的生活？要想過上這樣的生活，我們就必須要找出誰是控制者。那麼，控制者和被控制者是不同的嗎？如果它們是相同的，那也就沒有控制的必要了。

如果我心懷嫉妒，因為你什麼都有，自己卻一無所有而嫉妒你，這種嫉妒會引起憤怒、憎恨、妒忌和暴力意識：我希望擁有你所擁有的一切，如果得不到，我就會感到痛苦、憤怒。那麼，我有沒有可能過上沒有嫉妒的生活，不再進行比較？試試看。你能讓自己的生活中沒有任何比較嗎？我在挑選衣服時當然要做比較，但我說的並不是這種比較，而是指心理上沒有任何的量度和比較。如果不做任何量度，你會消亡嗎？會成為植物人嗎？會無事可做、陷入呆滯狀態嗎？

因為一直在比較，一直在掙扎，你才認為自己是活著的，但如果不再掙扎，那或許會是另外一種完全不同的生活形式。

第十六章 ｜ 神聖之事

你必須提出質疑，
不僅要質疑你的宗教導師，
而且還要質疑你自己，
不要盲從。
除了「眞理」的權威之外再沒有其他任何權威，
而這種眞理並非源于書本、思想或者牧師。

生活的藝術在於擁有完全的自由，這自由並不是選擇上的自由，不是想做什麼或喜歡做什麼就能去做的自由，因為那種自由是受環境、社會、宗教教義等因素影響的。我所說的自由是完全不同的。它不與任何事物相關，亦不源於任何事物。當存在這種自由的時候，生活中就不會再有衝突和問題。只要擁有自由，我們的大腦將完全活動起來──並不只是朝著某一個方向的活動，不管這個方向是科學上的、商業上的還是解決日常問題上的──智慧就會迅速成長，產生非比尋常的巨大能量。

　　從詞源上講，「自由」一詞也有愛的意思。討論自由，就要涉及關係問題。在一種關係中，你與對方不論是親密無間還是遠隔千里，只要你存有對方的影像，或者他對你存有影像，那就必會產生衝突。

　　視自由為選擇、運動、身份、地位、成就、成功的所有想法都是片面的，這些只是自由中微不足道的一部分。如果每個人都去做自己喜歡做的事，這樣的自由可能是最具破壞力的，並導致巨大的混亂——正如現在我們所看到的一樣。

我們祖祖輩輩生活在衝突之中，這種衝突並不僅僅存在於我們的關係中，也存在於我們與社會及其他國家之間。民族主義是一種部落崇拜，它導致了強烈的絕望、無窮的戰爭和分裂——分裂成猶太人和阿拉伯人，印度教徒和穆斯林，共產主義者、社會主義者和所謂的民主主義者。世界正在上演巨大的衝突，這就是人類創建的社會。

社會並非空中樓閣，它不是憑空產生的。我們所生活的社會是由所有人類共同創建，但其中存在著很多的不公平現象。我們創建了社會，卻又被它所束縛。除非出現一次徹底的變革、改變，除非從根本上發生一場心理革命——並非暴力革命（那會導致我們無處安身）——否則這個社會仍會保持當前的樣子。

改變意味著時間，從此處轉到彼處，從暴力轉向非暴力，需要漫長的時間。時間會改變人類嗎？這是一個非常基本的問題。在漫長的時間裡，在過去五千年乃至更多的時間裡，人類在心理上是否已經發生改變？顯然沒有。我們仍是非常原始的人，彼此爭吵，陷入無盡的戰爭與衝突。就心理、內在層面而言，我們的改變非常、非常少。也許從技術上講，我們發明了原子彈，製造出了性能卓越的機械和電腦，成就卓然，但從深層次的內在來看，我們仍保持著數千年前的樣子。時間並沒有改變人類。

人類爲什麼懼怕死亡？年老之後，人們要麼會加入某個教派，成爲非常虔誠的教徒或是變得非常迷信，要麼就開始探尋何爲死亡的問題。爲什麼我們會將生與死分離開來，爲什麼我們希望推遲死亡，希望死亡離自己越遠越好？人類這麼做，是因爲害怕失去已有的財富，進入未知的世界嗎？

生與死能否共存？請別急著回答。你要先理解什麼是生。眾所周知，生是一條恒久的道路，偶爾還伴隨著愉快、安逸的體驗，如果有錢的話，你多少還會產生一種安全感，但不安全感也會一直與你相伴。朝九晚五地上班，充滿著掙扎、競爭、爭吵、憎恨、愛（即所謂的快樂），這就是我們的生活方式。

雖然心裡明白，但人們還是會害怕失去一切。死亡意味著一切的終結——並不僅僅是有機體生命的結束，也意味著所有依戀、知識和經驗的結束。那麼，人能否與生死同行，而不是將兩者分離開來？也就是說，人能否放下自己的所有依戀，認同死亡？

死亡將會帶走你的一切：你的家人、知識、成就、聲名，你所擁有的一切。我們能否過一種與死亡同在的日常生活，放棄所有的依戀、競爭、心理成就，讓生與死之間不再存有任何間隔？這樣一來，你就會擁有莫大的自由和能量。但不要以爲因此就可以作惡、斂財、求取名聲，那些想法都是非常幼稚的，請原諒我用「幼稚」這個詞。當你能夠接受死亡，也就有了自由。

自遠古時代起，人類就一直在呆板、單調又機械化（生理上和心理上都是如此）地尋找超越生活之上的事物。人們認為那事物肯定存在。於是，他們便創造了神。神是思想創造出來的。但如果你心理上沒有絲毫的恐懼，那麼神對你來說還有意義嗎？

人一直在尋找神，牧師也就隨之而生。牧師們會說：「我們會為你講解，讓你認識它，你雖然無知，但我們是博學的。」其實不外乎是在服飾裝扮上下點工夫，給人留下深刻印象，再虛構一些天花亂墜般的神話場景。古埃及人，乃至比他們更為久遠的閃族人①，也相信存在天堂和地獄。他們說，你必須相信，否則就會下地獄。他們對那些不信仰者進行迫害、殺戮和折磨。基督教就是如此：你必須信仰耶穌，否則就是異端。在基督教的世界裡，懷疑是不被允許的。如果你開始懷疑，那麼所有的神話都會坍塌。但在亞洲，尤其是在印度，教義之一就是你必須提出質疑，不僅要質疑你的宗教導師，而且還要質疑你自己，不要盲從。在那裡，除了「真理」的權威之外再沒有其他任何權威，而這種真理並非源于書本、思想或者牧師。

什麼是宗教？如果拋棄了所有的荒謬言行、迷信和有組織的現代宗教信仰，如果你不再是一名印度教徒、佛教徒、基督教徒，那並不等於你就成了無神論者，而是意味著你正在探尋、質疑、詢問、討論、推斷、理解、思考。

---

①閃族人：起源于阿拉伯半　的游牧民族，又稱閃米特人，生活于大　七千年前。

那麼，是不是真的存在神聖的事物呢？有什麼事物是永恆的、超越時間的嗎？有什麼是思想未曾觸及的嗎？有些事物，是思想和「你」都不可能發現的。例如冥想，並不僅僅是重複念誦幾句咒語那麼簡單，那只是極不成熟的表現。冥想是不同尋常的事物，是對整個生命的理解——既包括外在的也包括內在的，是對你的日常生活及各種關係的理解，能使你免於恐懼；冥想也是對自我（即「我」）的質疑。「我」是否只是一個記憶的集合體，並因此而變得不真實？請認真思考這個問題。這也是冥想的一部分。

　　在梵語和普通字典裡，「冥想」一詞的意思是指內心擺脫了所有的標準。「我現在是這樣，我要變成那樣」就是一種標準。在科技領域，標準很重要。沒有標準，我們就無法發明發電機或原子彈，也沒法製造出汽車，但我們能否從心理、內在層面擺脫所有的比較與衡量標準？我們能否享受到那樣的自由：不再恐懼，不會再遭遇孩提時代起就受過的所有傷害，能夠遠離從前的心靈創傷，也不會再悲傷、痛苦、孤獨、沮喪、憂慮？我們能否擺脫自我、擺脫「我」——不是在生命結束之時，而是從現在開始，從聽到這些話的這一刻開始擺脫？

　　冥想是由大腦進行的具有重要意義的運動，而不是在壓制大腦。當大腦處於最佳狀態、充滿能量時，靜默就產生了。這種靜默不同于源於思想的靜，後者是受到局限的。只有當自由、愛和憐憫及至高的智慧存在時，才會進入這樣的靜默。但如果你依附於某個宗教、組織或皈依某種信仰，那就不可能擁有憐憫心或者愛。你必須是全然自由的，這種自由中存在著超越時間之上的空性（而非一無所有），其中蘊含著偉大的、巨大的能量。

這就是冥想。這就是宗教。

第十七章 │ 永 恒

在全然的靜默中，空無一物，
甚至你也不存在了。
心只有空無一物的時候，
才會完全地平和、安穩，
進而發現那種超越了時間概念、
難以描述的事物是否真的存在。

人們都在追求什麼？我認為這個問題非常值得探究，因為我們一直說自己在追求真理、追求愛，等等。可是如果你的心處於無序狀態，那又怎麼追求真理呢？所謂秩序，是讓萬物各就其位。當心處於迷茫、躊躇、疑惑、探索的狀態，想要尋求安全感或別的什麼東西時，這種欲望與不確定性必然會導致人們不可避免地產生錯覺與妄念，並使之成為心靈的依附。

你必須非常認真地探尋人類追求的是什麼，你我所追求的又是什麼。我們是否都希望得到幸福？之所以想要幸福，是不是因為現在不幸福，還處於痛苦、衝突、迷茫和極度焦慮中？我們是否因為如此，才會問「請告訴我如何才能過上幸福生活」？不幸的對立面，就是幸福嗎？如果你感到自己的生活充滿了不幸、憂傷、愁苦和焦慮，就會想要得到與此相反的生活：充滿明性、自由、幸福和秩序。我們的追求就是如此嗎？

請仔細聽我說。事物的對立面與事物本身一定是完全不同的嗎？或者，事物是根植于它的對立面？實際上，是人類創造了對立面。因此才有了白天與黑夜的區別，有了男人與女人的區別。但從心理、內在上來說，我們所希望得到的、追求的相反之物，其實就是現實的投射。比如說身處不幸的境地，人的反應自然是希望得到幸福。希望得到的事物源自于現實中正在發生的，僅此而已。

由此可見，對立面的事物總是來源於眞正的現實，因而是毫無意義的，眞正有意義的是現實。而人們因為不知道如何面對現實，所以建構了與之相對立的事物。如果知道如何應對正在發生的事，那麼對立面也就不復存在了。因此，理解現實遠比追求現實的對立面更重要。

為什麼我們會不幸福，會痛苦、爭吵，充滿暴力？為什麼會這樣？這就是現實。如果我知道如何改變現實，問題就會迎刃而解。我就是自己的導向燈，無須再追隨他人。那麼，不與對立面抗爭的話，我們有無可能解決現實的問題？實際上，只有當你擁有全部能量，即能量沒有浪費到衝突與鬥爭上時，你才有可能改變現實。我在不幸福的時候，會產生巨大的憂慮。這就是現實。偏離了它只會造成能量的浪費。我必須運用自己所擁有的全部能量，才能理解眞正的現實，並超越它。

秩序在生命中是必要的。我們說過，秩序就是將萬物置於合適的位置。但我們並不知道哪里是合適的位置。我們只知道無序，世界仍處於戰爭頻仍的無序狀態。現在，你的日常生活中是不是也存在無序？顯然存在，這是當前的現實。而我們想要秩序。我們認爲秩序是無序的對立面，這等於是在無序之外建立了秩序模式。我們在行爲舉止、思想和看法等方面都存在著無序，並認爲秩序就是現實對立面的藍圖。但是將秩序視爲藍圖必然會引起衝突，導致無序。哪里有衝突，哪里就有無序，比如國家的無序、政治的無序以及宗教的無序等等。

事實上，無序是必然存在的。現在，你能夠觀察和覺察到這種無序嗎？不要試圖改變它或壓制它，不要說「我必須找到無序之外的秩序」，而是要眞正覺察到你生命中的無序。這樣一來，你就會發現在那種無序中是有秩序的，而這秩序並非無序的對立面。

想知道是否存在終極眞理，就必須要有自由，避免受到權威與信仰的局限，這意味著不再有恐懼，因爲信仰源於恐懼和絕望。此外，還一定要有秩序。免于權威的自由、免于信仰的自由和秩序，這三者缺一不可。唯有如此，我們才能夠發現什麼是冥想。

什麼是冥想呢？爲什麼你應該冥想？冥想是一個與日常生活毫無關係的東西嗎？冥想需要練習嗎？是不是就像別人說的，冥想自成體系，需要每日練習和明確練習目標？雖然說熟能生巧，但那樣機械練習會讓你的心變得遲鈍、不敏感。這是顯而易見的，不是嗎？

我們通常所說的冥想，應是理解某些超越人類思想的事物，並從中得到啓迪的過程。你有沒有練習過冥想？有沒有練習過如何控制思想？有沒有問過誰是控制者這個問題？誰是思想的控制者？控制者與被控制者是不同的嗎？抑或控制者就是被控制者？人們通常都把控制者與被控制者區別開來看待，認爲是控制者控制了思想並試圖將它局限於特定的區域。但試圖控制思想的，不就是從思想實體中分離出來的另一種思想嗎？它們不都是思想嗎？

所謂冥想，是去理解思想應當處在什麼位置。冥想是不受任何控制的。你可曾嘗試過一種沒有任何控制的日常生活？理解這個問題時，你必須先瞭解爲什麼人會有一種要控制萬物、控制自己的思想和欲望的意識。爲什麼？而這就涉及到了注意力。

當你保持注意力，就會知道到底發生了什麼事：你正在建造一堵「抗拒之牆」，並將自己關入其中，認爲自己必須將注意力放在其上，而將其他一切事物置之度外，也就是說，你在運用自己的意志將思想控制在某些特定的區域上。而意志則是欲望的表露和本質。此外，在注意力之中，衝突仍在持續——每當神游四方，你就要將思想收回，並繼續保持專注。你從未問過爲什麼思想應該受控制。但如果你具有洞見，看到了思想應處的位置，那麼關於思想控制的問題將不復存在。

既然冥想沒有系統、無需練習、與控制思想無關，你就必須要找出保持專注的意義。專注意味著什麼？意味著沒有中心地觀察。這個中心就是「我」，就是「我」的欲望、成就與憂慮。當你集中了所有的注意力，即用上了全部的能量——包括你的神經、耳朵與眼睛，那麼在這種注意力中就不會有中心的存在，不會有「我」的存在。

現在，按照我所說的去做。你集中注意力了嗎？也就是說，你是不是在全神貫注地傾聽？聽！這意味著不去解讀，不去分析，不試圖去理解所說的話，只是傾聽。如果你能夠做到這一點，那麼頭腦中將不會有任何的思想運動，而只有傾聽。

這並不是你能在學校裡學到的。不是嗎？通過觀察、觀照自己對他人的反應方式，你會發現自己在生活中是否具有敏感的覺察力。因此，注意力是必要的。這同樣是冥想的一部分。

此外，冥想還意味著人處於完全平靜的狀態。這種平靜並非強制可得，因為強制獲得的平靜中存在著衝突——心依然在嘮叨、思考、傾聽並活動著。你會發現，只有當自己完全處於平靜狀態時，才能夠進行真正的觀察。

如果你想觀察山，觀察它們的倒影、光線、外在美與內涵，就會完全專注地去看。倘若走了神，那便是因為你並不在意。如果想要全神貫注地觀察某個事物，你的心會自然而然地趨於平靜，不是嗎？因此，當你去探求某個並非源於思想的事物時，一定會集中全部的注意力，這樣一來，你就會處於完全的安寧、平靜狀態。

大多數人都發現這很難做到，因為從生理上講，我們從未平靜過；我們的雙手、雙腳、雙眼從未有過片刻的停歇。總會有各種各樣的事情需要我們去做、去看。而我們從來都不曾瞭解過自己的身體。如果真的瞭解，你就會發現身體也有自己的智慧，這種智慧並非源於味覺、舌頭，或是對煙、酒、毒品的強制性欲望。

　　總之要想探求現實、探求真理，你就必須徹底摒棄所有的權威和信仰。這才是真正的秩序！如果心一直在喋喋不休地分析、探求，那便是對能量的浪費。當全然平靜下來，那便是心的重生。

　　前面說過，只有當心處於全然平靜的狀態，才有可能進行冥想，而這種平靜只能自然地形成，不是可以通過培養或練習得到的。如果你練習平靜，那麼它便不再是平靜而是死亡。你必須要明白這一點。同時，如果沒有憐憫，那麼你就不可能擁有平靜的心。因此，我們還必須探求愛是什麼。愛是快樂嗎？是欲望嗎？野心勃勃的人會有愛嗎？爭強好勝的人會有愛嗎？以自我為中心的人會有愛嗎？抑或，無我即是愛？當我仍是「我」時，當我只關注我自己的問題、野心、貪婪、妒忌、成功或欲望時，當我幻想自己是偉人、只關心我自己時，愛就不可能存在。愛意味著全然的憐憫。

　　心中有了愛，人就會完全處於平靜狀態。因為心中的一切都已經各就其位，處在應處的位置上，男人與女人之間的正確關係也就得以建立——這種關係並非基於影像、記憶或者曾經受過的傷害。

由此全然的專注和靜默得以產生。

那麼，這種靜默是怎樣的？靜默之時會發生什麼？有無可能描述它？這種靜默並非兩次噪音之間的間歇。沒有噪音並不等於真正的靜，就如同兩次戰爭之間的和平並非真正的和平一樣。假設你具有這般敏銳、超常的意識，能夠體會到真正的靜默之美，那麼明白當心完全靜默時會發生什麼事嗎？那時候，作爲量度標準的時間與思想的運動都將不復存在。

接下來我要說的你們可能不想聽，因爲在座的各位都是備受尊敬的人。當那種靜默出現時，一個絕對不存在任何事物的空間就會隨之而生。我要說的重點在於，其中沒有任何東西。你們明白我說的話嗎？各位都是有身份的人，不論是在自己的事業還是社會地位方面，你們都希望能夠獲得成就，都希望能夠有所得、有所實現。這無可厚非。但是在那種全然的靜默中，空無一物，你也不存在了。如果你依然存在其中的話，就不會有靜默，而只剩下噪音，你將無法傾聽或觀察。我們的心只有空無一物的時候，才會完全地平和、穩定。

唯有如此，心才會發現那種超越了時間概念、難以描述的事物是否真的存在。人必須過一種與他人的關係中沒有任何衝突的日常生活，因爲所有的關係即是生命的一部分。如果你不知道如何擁有與他人毫無衝突的關係，你的生命將會扭曲，變得醜陋、痛苦和虛假。

以上就是冥想的全部內容。唯有冥想，你才能發現什麼是永恆。

資料來源

- 第一章　生活就在當下

克氏1979年8月1日和15日的書信，《生命的整個運動是學習》，編輯雷·麥科伊（印度欽奈：克里希納穆提基金會，2006年），88-89頁，92頁。

- 第二章　思想是什麼

1973年3月11日克氏在美國加利福尼亞州三藩市的公開演講。

- 第三章　死亡的意義

1982年2月6日克氏在印度孟買的公開演講。

- 第四章　理解愛

1985年7月25日克氏在瑞士薩嫩市的公開對話。

- 第五章　傾聽、觀察與學習

1977年4月10日克氏在美國加利福尼亞州奧哈伊鎮的公開演講。

- 第六章　冥想的基礎

1979年1月7日克氏在印度馬德拉斯市的公開演講。

- 第七章　專注

1984年8月28日克氏在英國布魯克伍德公園的公開問答部分。

- 第八章　不再恐懼

1977年7月14日克氏在瑞士薩嫩市的公開演講。

● 第九章　喚醒所有的感覺
1983年5月17日克氏在美國加利福尼亞州奧哈伊鎮的公開問答。

● 第十章　愛、自由、良善與美麗
1984年2月12日克氏在印度孟買市的公開演講。

● 第十一章　冥想的祝福
1968年11月17日克氏在美國克雷爾蒙特大學的公開演講，《與美國學生的對話》（波士頓：香巴拉出版社，1988年），122-130頁。

● 第十二章　偉大的生命
1984年1月7日克氏在印度馬德拉斯市的公開演講。

● 第十三章　死亡的藝術
1984年2月11日克氏在印度孟買市的公開演講。

● 第十四章　觀察是唯一的真理
1968年1月3日克氏在印度馬德拉斯市的公開演講，《智慧的覺醒》（倫敦：維克多·戈蘭茨公司，1980年），186-196頁。

● 第十五章　自由自在的生命
1978年7月28日克氏在瑞士薩嫩市的公開演講。

● 第十六章　神聖之事
1984年4月15日克氏在美國紐約州紐約市的公開演講。

● 第十七章　永恆
1975年4月20日克氏在美國加利福尼亞州奧哈伊鎮的公開演講。
可訪問www.jkrishnamurti.com，瞭解克里希納穆提和克里希納穆提基金會的更多資訊。

附錄

（原文）

THE POCKET KRISHNAMURTI

EDITOR'S INTRODUCTION

The Art of Living

Do we sometimes feel that we waste our lives, that they are without meaning, full of conflict and confusion around us and within us? In this collection, comprised mostly of unpublished talks in California, England, and Switzerland, Krishnamurti considers these feelings, and suggests that there is a way of living daily life that is entirely different from what it normally is—a way of living without any control, without any conflict, yet without conformity. He says that life can have great beauty and significance if there is clear observation of what is actually happening in our actions and reactions, in our relationships. Human beings have tremendous capacity but we are conditioned to solve problems; this denies freedom. When we recognize our conditioning, Krishnamurti explains, we reject psychological authority, and may then observe and act with greater clarity. With observation free of words and thought, we can see that freedom, love, beauty, and goodness are one, not separate.

Krishnamurti speaks of an art of living a life in which there is no conflict whatsoever, one that is totally free of fear, including the fear of death. We can understand the root of fear and the cause of sorrow if we look at our conditioning. In this way we see that thought is a process of time and memory that interferes with direct perception. Understanding what prevents order in consciousness, and so in our lives, depends on the arts of listening, seeing, and learning. Krishnamurti discusses each of these in simple words with the freshness of truth.

In these talks, which Krishnamurti described as conversations between us and him, there is a quality of meditation in which we may glimpse a timeless emptiness that is, perhaps, sacred, with meaning beyond words.

Ray McCoy

[1]

LIFE IS WHAT IS HAPPENING THIS INSTANT

THE GREATEST ART is the art of living, greater than all things that human beings have created by mind or hand, greater than all the scriptures and their gods. It is only through this art of living that a new culture can come into being. This art of living can come only out of total freedom.

This freedom is not an ideal, a thing to take place eventually. The first step in freedom is the last step in it. It is the first step that counts, not the last step. What you do now is far more essential than what you do at some future date. Life is what is happening this instant, not an imagined instant, not what thought has conceived, so it is the first step you take now that is important. If that step is in the right direction, then the whole of life is open to you. The right direction is not toward an ideal, a predetermined end, it is inseparable from what is taking place now. This is not a philosophy as a series of theories; it is exactly what the word *philosophy* means, the love of truth, the love of life. It is not something that you go to a university to learn. We are learning about the art of living in our daily life.

As life is so complex, it is always difficult and confusing to pick one aspect and say it is the most important. The very choice, the differentiating quality, leads to further confusion. If you say this is the most important, then you relegate the other facts of life to a secondary position. Either we take the whole movement of life as one, which becomes extremely difficult for most people, or we take one fundamental aspect in which all the others may be included. Let us go into it very slowly and hesitantly.

We are exploring together one facet of life, and in the very understanding of it we may cover the whole field of life. To investigate, we must be free of our prejudices, personal experiences, and predetermined conclusions. Like a good scientist, we must have a mind unclouded by knowledge that we have already accumulated. We must come to it afresh, without any reaction to what is being observed. This is absolutely necessary; otherwise investigation is colored by our own fears, hopes, and pleasures. The very urge to investigate, and the intensity of it, frees the mind from its coloring.

One of the most important things is the art of living. Is there a way of living our daily life that is entirely different from what it normally is? Is there a way of living without any control, without any conflict, without a disciplinary conformity? I can find out only when my whole mind is facing exactly what is happening now. This means I can find out what it means to live without conflict only when what is happening *now* can be observed.

This observation is not an intellectual or emotional affair but acute, clear, sharp perception in which there is no duality, no opposition or contradiction in what is going on. Duality arises only when there is an escape from *what is*. This escape creates the opposite and so conflict arises. There is only the actual and nothing else.

Associations and reactions to what is happening are the conditioning of the mind. This conditioning prevents the observation of what is taking place now. What is taking place now is free of time. Time is the evolution of our conditioning. It is humanity's inheritance, the burden that has no beginning. When there is this passionate observation of what is going on, that which is being observed dissolves into nothingness. An observation of anger that is taking place now reveals the whole nature and structure of violence. This insight is the ending of all violence.

Anger has many stories behind it. It is not just a solitary event. It has a great many associations. These very associations, with their emotions, prevent actual observation. With anger the content is the anger. The anger is the content; they are not two separate things. The content is the conditioning. In the passionate observation of what is actually going on—that is, of the activities of the conditioning—the nature and structure of the conditioning are dissolved.

It is really simple, so simple that you miss its very simplicity and so its subtlety. What we are saying is that whatever is happening, when you are walking, talking, meditating, the event that is taking place is to be observed. When the mind wanders, the very observation of it ends its chatter. So there is no distraction whatsoever at any time.

Remembrance has no place in the art of living. Relationship is the art of living. If there is remembrance in relationship, it is not relationship. Relationship is between human beings, not their memories. It is these memories that divide, and so there is contention, the opposition of the "you" and the "me." So thought, which is remembrance, has no place whatsoever in relationship. This is the art of living.

Relationship is to all things, to nature, the birds, the rocks—to everything around us and above us—to the clouds, the stars, and the blue sky. All existence is relationship; without it you cannot live. Because we have corrupted relationship, we live in a society that is degenerating.

The art of living can come into being only when thought does not contaminate love.

[2]

WHAT DO WE WANT?

I WONDER if you have ever considered how we waste our life, how we dissipate our energies, how intellectually we are secondhand people. There is nothing but routine, boredom, loneliness, suffering, either physiologically or psychologically. Our life, as it is lived now, unfortunately has no meaning whatsoever, except to earn a livelihood, which is obviously necessary. Besides that, our whole life is fragmented, broken up, and a mind that is broken up, fragmented, is a corrupt mind. The word *corrupt* means broken up.

What is it that we want? What is it that we have achieved? What is it that we have become? For most of us, life is travail, strife. In this particular society, to be successful in it is to make money. We are either seeking power, position, prestige, or living a bourgeois, narrow, shallow, empty life, filled with all kinds of opinions, judgments, beliefs. All that seems such a wasteful life. We are never happy except in the pursuit of pleasure, from which we derive a certain sense of enjoyment, a certain sense of gratification, satisfaction. But when you examine a little more deeply into yourself, apart from what you have learned from books, and from the reactions of the country in which you live, don't you find that there is absolutely nothing inward except what you have put into it? What you have put into it is the fabrication of thought. And thought does not bring about the total action of a human being. It is only a partial, fragmentary action.

Realizing that our life, as it is, is empty, rather shallow, and sorrowful, we escape into various pursuits of pleasure, religious pleasure or so-called worldly pleasure, seeking money, greater enjoyment, greater pleasures, buying more things, maintaining a society of consumerism and ultimately ending in the grave. That is our life, and there is nothing sacred, there is nothing really religious.

Life is dreadfully serious, and it is only those who are really deeply serious who *live*. Those who are flippant seek the entertainment of the gurus or the priests, or the intellectual philosophers, and *they* become our life through words without substance, descriptions without the described.

So one asks: what is the place of thought in our life? All our civilization, our culture, is based on thought. Religions are the product of thought; behavior, conduct, the business world, relationship, the accumulation of armaments, the army, the navy, the air force are all based on thought. Whether the thought is reasonable or unreasonable, logical or illogical, sane or neurotic, our action is based on thought as an idea, thought as an ideal. We are all terribly idealistic, most unfortunately. The ideal is not *what is*; the ideal is something invented by thought as a means to overcome *what is*. There is division between that ideal and *what is*, and so, conflict.

I hope you are not merely hearing a series of words but actually observing the whole movement of your own mind so that we can establish a relationship, a communication in which we understand what we are talking about, without agreement or disagreement but merely observing what actually is.

One must go into what thought is and what thinking is. You know, it is one of the most extraordinary things that the whole of Asia considers thought to be the child of a barren woman. They say thought is measure, and to find the immeasurable, that which is beyond time and measure, one must pursue the suppression of thought. Whereas the whole of Western civilization, culture, is based on thought. Thought is measurement.

As I said, this is really very serious, and it requires great subtlety of mind to go into it. I hope you are prepared to investigate this so that the mind is free from measurement, so that the mind knows vast space and silence, which is not measurable, which is not put together by thought.

We are saying that the culture of Western civilization is based on thought, on measurement. From that measurement has grown the whole technological world and the art of war; and in that world, religion is a matter of belief, acceptance, propaganda, saviors, and so on. In the East they use thought to go beyond thought, and in the West they have accepted measurement, progress, and a way of life that is based on technology, acquiring more and more enjoyment, and having great pleasure in possessions, including literature and poetry.

A serious mind must ask what place thought has in life. What is the function of thought, thought that is either sane, logical, reasoned; or that has perverted life, giving importance to *things*, to property, to money, to pleasure; thought, which has accumulated so much information, both outwardly and inwardly? What is the place of thought and what is its relationship to action? Because life is action; relationship is movement in action. Is there an action in life that is not bound by time and thought and measure?

To live is to act. Whatever we do is action, and if that action is bound by the past through the present to the future, then action is never liberating, then action is always fragmentary. And such action is corruption.

So what is action, and what is its relationship to thought? Thought is the response of memory, as knowledge and experience, stored in the brain. You don't have to read neurological or scientific books, you can observe it in yourself if you are deeply interested in it. Without memory you cannot act, you cannot remember words; you then become in a state of amnesia, complete confusion. And thought responds to any challenge according to its conditioning. If you are a Christian or a Hindu or a Buddhist or a communist or a capitalist, your mind is conditioned in that, and you act according to that conditioning. That conditioning is the memory, the experience, the knowledge of that particular culture or society in which you live. That is fairly obvious, isn't it? So thought in action is separative, fragmentary, and brings about conflict.

We must understand this, because we are trying to find a way of life in which there is no conflict whatsoever, a way of life in which there is no sorrow, a way of life that is total, complete, whole, harmonious, sane. And thought may be one of the factors that brings about fragmentation and therefore corruption. Therefore one must find out what the function of thought is and what place thought has in human relationship.

One can see very clearly that thought in the field of technology is essential. In the field of knowledge, thought can function logically, sanely, objectively, efficiently. But that efficiency, sanity, objectivity becomes polluted when thought seeks status through technology. When the mind seeks status through technological function, then inevitably there must be conflict and therefore corruption. That is obvious. But your conditioning is so strong that you will pursue status in spite of logical, sane, rational thinking. You will pursue status, and therefore continue with conflict and therefore corruption. Corruption is not merely taking money from another, or doing ugly things; the deep cause of corruption is when thought breaks up action into' fragments—intellectual action, emotional action, physical action, or ideological action.

So, is there an action in human relationship that is not fragmentary but whole? Is there an action that is not controlled by thought or by measurement or by the past? Action is also when you say a word, when you make a gesture of contempt or of welcome; action may be going from here to there. There is action according to a formula, action according to an opinion, action according to an idea, an ideal, or action based on some neurotic or rational belief. It is either acting according to a past pattern, or acting according to a future abstraction.

The most fundamental thing in life is relationship. Behavior, virtue, conduct, and society are born from relationship. And thought is measurement, conformity, acting according to a particular conclusion, from knowledge that is always in the past. What place has thought in human relationship? Or has it no place at all? If it has a place in human relationship, then thought limits, controls relationship, and therefore in that relationship there is fragmentation and hence conflict.

There are two principles on which our life is based: pleasure and fear. Please observe it in yourself. Pleasure has become tremendously important in life. There are various forms of pleasure: sexual pleasure, intellectual pleasure, the pleasure of possession, the pleasure of money, the pleasure of power, prestige, the pleasure of self-importance, the pleasure that you derive when the "me," the ego, asserts itself through domination and so on, or accepts tyranny as a means of achievement. And in relationship, pleasure takes the form of dependency. You depend on another psychologically in relationship. Where there is dependence there must be fear of losing, and therefore greater attachment. The pursuit of pleasure sexually is fairly obvious. Most extraordinarily, this pleasure has become the most important thing in life. There is the pleasure of dependence, depending on another psychologically because in oneself one is frightened of being alone, is lonely, desperate, not having love or not being loved, and so on. So there is the pursuit of pleasure and the constant avoidance of fear. And thought sustains both: you think about the pleasure that you have had yesterday, and you hope to have it again today. And if that pleasure is not continued, you get violent, anxious, fearful. Observe this in yourself.

And there is the whole question of fear. A life that is lived in fear is a dark, ugly life. Most of us are frightened in different ways. Can the mind be totally free of fear? Nobody wants to be free of pleasure but you all want to be free of fear; you don't see that both of them go together, that they are two sides of the same coin, sustained by thought. That is why it is very important to understand thought. You know we have fears: fear of death, fear of life, fear of darkness, fear of our neighbor, fear of ourself, fear of losing a job, and the deeper unconscious layers of fear hidden in the deep recesses of our own mind. There is insecurity and so, seeking security. Is it possible for the mind to be free of fear totally, so the mind is really free to enjoy life—not to pursue pleasure but to enjoy life? It is not possible to enjoy life as long as fear exists.

Will analysis dispel fear? Or is analysis a form of paralyzing the mind not to have freedom from fear? See the implication of it. You are used to analysis; that is one of the intellectual forms of entertainment. In analysis, there is the analyzer and the analyzed, whether the analyzer is a professional or you. When there is analysis, there is division between the analyzer and the analyzed, and hence conflict. And in analysis you need time; you take days, years, and that gives you an opportunity to postpone action. You can analyze the whole problem of violence indefinitely, seeking its cause, hearing the explanations of different professionals about what the causes of violence are, reading volumes about the causes of violence and analyzing them. All that takes time, and in the meantime you can enjoy your violence. Analysis implies division and postponement of action—and therefore analysis brings more conflict, not less. Analysis implies time.

A mind that observes the truth of this is free of analysis, and therefore is capable of directly dealing with violence, which is what is. If you observe totally, without analysis, violence in yourself—violence brought about through fear, through insecurity, through the sense of loneliness, dependency, through the cutting off of your pleasures, and so on—then you have all the energy that has been dissipated through analysis to go beyond *what is*.

Can the deep-rooted fears given to us by the society in which we live, inherited from the past, all be exposed so that the mind is completely free of this terrible thing called fear? Can one observe the totality of fear, or only the branches of fear, not the very root of fear, the cause of fear? Can the mind observe, see, be aware of, give total attention to fear, whether it is hidden, put away deeply in the recesses of one s own mind, or seen in the outward expressions of daily fears— like the fear of the pain of yesterday coming back again today or tomorrow? The fear of losing a job, the fear of being insecure outwardly as well as inwardly, the ultimate fear of death—there are so many forms of fear. Should we cut away each branch or come to grips with the totality of fear? Is the mind capable of observing fear totally?

We are used to dealing with fear in fragments. I am afraid of this or that; I am afraid of losing a job, or afraid of my wife, or my husband; I am concerned with fragments and not with the totality of fear. To observe the totality of fear is to give complete attention when any fear arises.

You know, we look at anger or jealousy, envy, fear, or pleasure as an observer wanting to get rid of it. There is always an observer, a seer, a thinker, so we look at fear as though we were outside looking in. Now, can you observe fear without the observer? The observer is the past. The observer recognizes the reaction that it calls *fear* in terms of the past, and names it as fear. The observer is always looking from the past at the present, and so there is a division between the observer and the observed. Can you observe fear without the reaction to that as the past, which is the observer?

Look, I have met you in the past and you have insulted me, flattered me. You have done a great many things for me and against me. All that is the accumulated memory that is the past. The past is the observer, is the thinker, and when he or she looks at you, he or she is looking with the eyes of the past and does not look at you afresh. So the observer never sees you properly, he or she only sees you with the eyes that have already been corrupted, that have already been dulled. So can you observe fear without the past? That means not to name the fear, not to use the word fear at all, but just to observe. That totality of attention is possible only when there is no observer, which is the past. When you do that, when you observe totally, then the whole content of consciousness as fear is dissipated.

There is fear from outside and from within. I fear that my son may get killed in a war. War is external, the invention of technology, which has developed such monstrous instruments of destruction. Inwardly I cling to my son; I love him, and I have educated him to conform to the society in which he lives, which says to kill. We have built a society that is so corrupt, that is so immoral. It is concerned only with possessing more and more, with consumerism. It is not concerned with the total development of the world, of human beings.

You know, we have no compassion. We have a great deal of knowledge, a great deal of experience. We can do extraordinary things medically, technologically, scientifically, but we have no compassion whatsoever. Compassion means passion for all human beings, and animals, nature. How can there be compassion when there is fear, when the mind is constantly pursuing pleasure? You want pleasure; you want to control fear, put it underground; and you also want compassion. You want it all, but you cannot have it. You can have compassion only when fear is not. And that is why it is so important to understand fear in our relationship. That fear can be totally uprooted when you can observe the reaction without naming it. The very naming of it is the projection of the past. So thought sustains and pursues pleasure, and thought also gives strength to fear—I am afraid of what might happen tomorrow, I am afraid of losing a job, I am afraid of time as death.

So thought is responsible for fear. And we live in thought, our daily activity is based on thought. What place has thought in human relationship? You have insulted me; that leaves a memory, that leaves a mark as memory in my mind, and I look at you with that memory. Or if you flatter me, I look at you with that memory. So I have never looked at you without the eyes of the past. So it is very important to understand what place thought has in relationship. If it has a place, then relationship is daily routine, mechanical, with meaningless pleasure and fear.

Then one comes to the question: what is love? Is it the product of thought? Unfortunately it has been made the product of thought—we "love" God and "love" man—and destroy nature. One must go into this question deeply to find out for oneself what love is, because without that, without that quality of compassion, we will always suffer. And to come upon it, for the mind to have that deep compassion, one must understand suffering, for passion is the outcome of suffering. The root meaning of the word *passion* is sorrow, suffering; and most of us escape from suffering. It is not that we must accept physical and psychological suffering. That is silly. But is thought the movement of suffering? Or is suffering something entirely different from thought? It is immensely important to understand the machinery of thinking, not verbally understand it but actually observe in ourselves what thinking is, and see what its relationship is to our daily life.

[3]

THE FULL SIGNIFICANCE OF DEATH

THE AVERAGE PERSON wastes his life. He has a great deal of energy but he wastes it. He spends his days in the office, or in digging the garden, or as a lawyer, or he leads the life of a sannyasin. The life of an average person seems, at the end, utterly meaningless, without significance. When he looks back, when he is fifty, eighty, or ninety, he asks what he has done with his life.

Life has a most extraordinary significance, with its great beauty, its great suffering and anxiety. At the end of it all, what have we done with life? Money, sex, the constant conflict of existence, the weariness, the travail, unhappiness, and frustrations are all we have, with perhaps occasional joy; or perhaps you love someone completely, wholly, without any sense of self.

There seems to be so little justice in the world. Philosophers have talked a great deal about justice. The social workers talk about justice. The average person wants justice. But is there justice in life at all? One is clever, well placed, with a good mind, and is good-looking, having everything he or she wants. Another has nothing. One is well educated, sophisticated, free to do what he or she wants. Another is a cripple, poor in mind and in heart. One is capable of writing and speaking, and is a good human being. Another is not. One is fair, another is dark. One is bright, aware, sensitive, full of feeling, loving a beautiful sunset, the glory of the moon, the astonishing light on the water; one sees all that, and another does not. One is reasonable, sane, healthy, and another is not.

So one asks, seriously, is there justice in the world at all? Can human beings ever have justice? When one looks around, life seems so empty and meaningless for most people. Before the law all are supposedly equal, but some are more equal than others who have not sufficient money to employ good lawyers. Some are born high, others low. This has been the problem of philosophy, the love of truth, love of life. But perhaps truth is in life, not in books, not in ideas, not separate from fife. Perhaps truth is where we are and in how we live.

As we observe all this in the world, there is apparently very little justice.

So where is justice then? It appears that there is justice only when there is compassion. Compassion is the ending of suffering. Compassion is not born out of tiny religion or from belonging to any cult. You cannot have your superstitions and invented gods and become compassionate. To have compassion there must be complete and total freedom from all conditioning. Is such freedom possible?

The human brain has been conditioned over millions of years. That is a fact. And it seems that the more knowledge we acquire about all the things of the earth and heavens, the more we get bogged down. When there is compassion, then with it there is intelligence, and that intelligence has the vision of justice. We have invented the ideas of karma and reincarnation, and we think that by inventing those ideas, those systems about something that is to happen in the future, we have solved the problem of justice. Justice begins only when the mind is very clear and when there is compassion.

Our brains are very complex instruments. Your brain, or my brain, is of the brain of humanity. It has not just developed from when we were born until now. It has evolved through endless time and conditions our consciousness. That consciousness is not personal, it is the ground on which all human beings stand. When you observe this consciousness with all its content of beliefs, dogmas, concepts, fears, pleasures, agonies, loneliness, depression, and despair, it is not your individual consciousness. It is not that the individual holds this consciousness. We are deeply conditioned to think that we are separate individuals, but it is not your brain or mine. We are not separate.

Our brains are so conditioned through education, through religion, to think we are separate entities with separate souls and so on. We are not individuals at all. We are the result of thousands of years of human experience, human endeavor and struggle. So, we are conditioned; therefore we are never free. As long as we live with or by a concept, a conclusion, with certain ideas or ideals, our brains are not free and therefore there is no compassion. Where there is freedom from all conditioning, which is freedom from being a Hindu, a Christian, a Muslim, or a Buddhist, freedom from being caught up in specialization (though specialization has its place), freedom from giving one's life entirely to money, then there can be compassion.

As long as the brain is conditioned, as it is now, there is no freedom for humanity. There is no ascent through knowledge, as some philosophers and biologists are saying. Knowledge is necessary to drive a car, to do business, to go somewhere, to bring about technological development, and so on. But the psychological knowledge that one has gathered about oneself, which culminates in memory, is the result of external pressures and inward demands, and is not necessary.

Our lives are broken up, fragmented, divided. They are never whole; we never have holistic observation. We observe from a particular point of view. We are in ourselves broken up so that our lives are in contradiction in themselves; therefore there is constant conflict. We never look at life as a whole, complete and indivisible. The word *whole* means to be healthy, to be sane; it also means holy. That word has great significance. It is not that the various fragmented parts become integrated in our human consciousness. We are always trying to integrate various contradictions. But is it possible to look at life as a whole, to see the suffering, the pleasure, the pain, the tremendous anxiety, the loneliness, going to the office, having a house, sex, having children, as though they were not separate activities, but a holistic movement, a unitary action? Is that possible at all? Or must we everlastingly live in fragmentation and therefore be forever in conflict?

Is it possible to observe the fragmentation and the identification with those fragments? To observe, not correct, not transcend, not run away from or suppress, but observe. It is not a matter of what to do about it because, if you attempt to do something about it, you are then acting from a fragment and therefore cultivating further fragments and divisions. Whereas, if you can observe holistically the whole movement of life as one, then not only does conflict with its destructive energy cease, but also out of that observation comes a totally new approach to life.

I wonder if one is aware of how broken up one's daily life is? And if one is aware, does one then ask how to bring it all together to make a whole? And who is the entity, the "I," who is to bring all these various parts together and integrate them? Isn't that entity also a fragment? Thought itself is fragmentary, because knowledge is never complete about anything. Knowledge is accumulated memory, and thought is the response of that memory, and therefore it is limited. Thought can never bring about a holistic observation of life.

So, can one observe the many fragments that are our daily life and look at them as a whole? One is a professor, or a teacher, or a householder, or a sannyasin who has renounced the world; those are fragmented ways of living a daily life. Can one observe the whole movement of one's fragmented life with its separate and separative motives? Can one observe them all without the observer? The observer is the past, the accumulation of memories. The observer is that past and that is time. The past is looking at this fragmentation; and the past, as memory, is also in itself the result of previous fragmentations.

So, can one observe without time, without thought, without the remembrances of the past, and without the word? Because the word is the past, the word is not the thing. One is always looking through words, through explanations, which are movements of words. We never have a direct perception. Direct perception is insight that transforms the brain cells themselves. One's brain has been conditioned through time and functions in thinking. It is caught in that cycle. When there is pure observation of any problem, there is a transformation, a mutation, in the very structure of the cells.

We have created psychological time as hope, time as achievement. We are masters of that inward time that thought has put together. That is why we must understand the nature of time, which man has created. Why have human beings, psychologically, inwardly, created time—time when one will be good; time when one will be free of violence; time to achieve enlightenment; time to achieve some exalted state of mind; time as meditation? When one functions within the realm of that time, one is bringing about a contradiction and hence conflict. Psychological time is conflict.

It is really a great discovery if one realizes the truth that one is the past, the present, and the future, which is time as psychological knowledge. This creates a division in our consciousness between our living and the distant time that is death. That is, one is living with all one's problems, and death is something to be avoided, postponed, put at a great distance, that is another fragmentation in one's life. To observe holistically the whole movement of life is to live both the living and the dying. But one clings to life and avoids death; one does not even talk about it. So not only has one fragmented one's life, superficially, physically, but also one has separated oneself from death.

What is death? Is it not part of one's life? One may be frightened, one may want to avoid death and to prolong living, but always at the end of it there is death.

What is living? What is living, which is our consciousness? Consciousness is made up of its content; and the content is not different from consciousness.

Consciousness is what one believes, one's superstitions, the gods, the rituals; one's greed, ambitions, competitiveness; the depth of one's loneliness, attachment, suffering. All that is one's consciousness, which is oneself. But that consciousness is not one's own; it is the consciousness of humanity. One is the world and the world is oneself. One is one's consciousness with its content.

That content is the ground upon which all humanity stands. Therefore, psychologically, inwardly, one is not an individual. Outwardly one may have a different form from another, be yellow, brown, black, tall or short, be a woman or a man, but inwardly, deeply, we are similar, perhaps with some variations, but the similarity is like a string that holds the pearls together.

We must comprehend what living is, then we can ask what dying is. What is before death is more important than what happens after death. Before the end, long before the last minute, what is living? Is living the travail and conflict without any relationship with each other? Is the sense of deep, inward loneliness what we call living? To escape from this so-called living, you go off to churches, temples, pray and worship, which is utterly meaningless. If you have money you indulge in extravagance. You know all the tricks you play to escape from your own consciousness, from your own state of mind. And this is what is called living.

Death is the ending of everything that you know. It is the ending of every attachment—all the money you have accumulated, which you cannot take with you—therefore you are frightened. Fear is part of your life. And so whatever you are, however rich, however poor, however highly placed, whatever power you have, there is the ending, which is called death.

And what is it that is dying? It is the "me" with all the accumulations that it has gathered in this life, all the pain, the loneliness, the despair, the tears, the laughter, the suffering that is the "me" with all its words. The summation of all this is "me." I may pretend that I have in me some higher spirit, the atman, the soul, something everlasting, but that is all put together by thought. And thought is not sacred.

So our life is this "me" that you cling to, to which you are attached. And the ending of that is death. It is the fear of the known, and the fear of the unknown. The known is our life, and we are afraid of that life; and the unknown is death, of which we are also afraid.

Death is the total denial of the past, present, and the future, which is "me."

And being frightened of death, you think there are other lives to be lived. You believe in reincarnation; that is a nice, happy projection of comfort, invented by people who have not understood what living is. They see living is pain, constant conflict, endless misery with an occasional flare of smile, laughter, and joy, and they say, "We will live again next life; after death I will meet my wife or husband, my son, my god." Yet we have not understood what we are and what we are attached to. One has to inquire very closely and deeply into one's attachment. Death does not permit one to have anything when one dies.

Can the brain, the human consciousness, be free of this fear of death? As one is the master of psychological time, can one live with death and not keep it separate as something to be avoided, to be postponed, something to be put away? Death is part of life. Can one live with death and understand the meaning of ending? That is to understand the meaning of negation; ending one's attachments, ending one's beliefs, by negating. When one negates, ends, there is something totally new. So, while living, can one negate attachment completely? That is living with death.

Death is an ending and has extraordinary importance in life. Not suicide, not euthanasia, but the ending of one's attachments, one's pride, one's antagonism or hatred for another. When one looks holistically at life, then the dying, the living, the agony, the despair, the loneliness, and the suffering are all one movement. When one sees holistically there is total freedom from death. There is a sense of ending and therefore there is no continuity; there is freedom from the fear of not being able to continue, even though the body will be destroyed.

When one human being understands the full significance of death, there is the vitality, the fullness, that lies behind that understanding; he is out of the human consciousness. Life and death are one when you begin to end in living; then you are living side by side with death. When you understand that, it is the most extraordinary thing to do. There is neither the past nor the present nor the future, there is only the ending.

[4]

UNDERSTAND WHAT LOVE IS

THOUGHT IS associated with other thoughts, it is a series of movements that we call thinking. One thought cannot exist by itself; there is not one thought without all the associations in connection with it. And thinking is the very life of us; that is so obvious. Thought is always in relation to something, and in pursuing one thought, other thoughts arise. I am polishing my shoes and look out of the window and see the mountains, and I am off! And I have to come back to polishing my shoes. I want to concentrate on something and the thought shoots off in another direction. I pull it back and try to concentrate. This goes on all the time from childhood until we die. And the more I think about thought, the more thought there is: "I shouldn't think along those lines, I must think rightly"; "Is there right thinking, is there wrong thinking, is there purposeful thinking?"; "What is the purpose of my life?"; and so on. The whole process of thinking begins and there is no end to it.

Thought has done the most extraordinary things. Technologically, it has done the most appalling things, terrifying things. It has built all the rituals of every religion, and it has tortured human beings. It has expelled people from one part of the world to another. Thought, whether Eastern or Western, is still thinking; it is not Eastern thinking and Western thinking, two separate things.

Is there an end to thought? Not to your way of thinking, or my way of thinking, and all of us thinking together, moving in the same direction. We are asking whether thought can ever stop. That is, is there an end to time? Thinking is the result of knowledge, memory. To acquire knowledge, one needs time. Even the computer, which is so extraordinary, has to be given a split second before it gallops out what it wants to say. So when we are asking whether thought can ever end, we are also asking whether there is a stop to time. It is a rather interesting question if you go into it.

What does time mean to us, not only psychologically but outwardly—sunset, sunrise, learning a language, and so on? You need time to go from here to there, even by the fastest train or airplane. As long as there is a distance between what is and what might be, what I am and what I will be, whether it is a very short distance or centuries of distance, that distance can only be covered in time. So time implies evolution. You plant the seed in the earth; it takes a whole season to mature, grow, or a thousand years to become a full tree. Everything that grows or becomes needs time. Everything. So time and thought are not two separate movements. They are one solid movement.

We are asking whether thought and time have an end, a stop. How will you find out? This has been one of the problems confronting the human being from the beginning. This movement of time is a circle; time is a bondage. Hope involves time. So man has asked not if there is timelessness but rather if there is an end to time.

This is really a very serious question, We are not inquiring into the timeless. We are asking whether time, which is thought, has a stop. Now, how will you discover that? Through analysis? Through so-called intuition? That word, *intuition*, which has been used so much, may be most dangerous. It may be our hidden desire; it may be our deeply rooted motive of which we are not aware; it may be the prompting of our tendency, our own idiosyncrasy, our own particular accumulation of knowledge. We are asking, if you put all that aside, has time a stop? How will you find out? You, not anybody else, because what others say has no importance.

We have to inquire very deeply into the nature of time just as we went very deeply into the nature of thinking. Can all that come to an end? Is it a gradual process? If it is a gradual process, the very gradualness is time, so the ending cannot be gradual; it cannot be "eventually." It cannot be next weekend or tomorrow, or a few minutes later. It cannot be the next second either. All that allows time. If one really grasps all this, deeply comprehends the nature of thought, the nature of time, discipline, the art of living—if one does not cover it up by all kinds of movements but stays with it quietly—then there is a glimpse of its nature, an insight into it that is not related to memory, to anything. Find out!

The speaker can easily say there is an ending. That would be too childish. Unless we actually investigate, experiment, push it, go into it deeply, we cannot come upon a strange sense of timelessness.

How can our limited brain grasp the unlimited? It cannot, because it is limited. Can we grasp the significance, the depth, of the quality of the brain and recognize the fact—the fact, not the idea—that our brains are limited by knowledge, by specialities, by particular disciplines, by belonging to a group, a nationality? That is basically self-interest, camouflaged, hidden, by all kinds of things—robes, crowns, rituals. Essentially, this limitation comes into being when there is self-interest. That is so obvious. When I am concerned with my own happiness, with my own fulfilment, with my own success, that very self-interest limits the quality of the brain and the energy of the brain. That brain, for millions of years, has evolved in time, death, and thought. Evolution means a whole series of time events. To put all the religious rituals together needs time. So the brain has been conditioned, limited by its own volition, seeking its own security, keeping to its own backyard, saying, "I believe," "I don't believe," "I agree," "I don't agree," "This is my opinion," "This is my judgment." It is all self-interest, whether it is in the hierarchy of religion, or among the various noted politicians, or the person who seeks power through money, or the professor with his or her tremendous scholastic knowledge, or all the gurus who are talking about goodness, peace. It is all part of self-interest.

Our brain has become very small; we have reduced the quality of its immense capacity. Technologically, it has made tremendous improvements, and it also has immense capacity to go inwardly very, very deeply. But self-interest limits it. To discover for oneself where self-interest is hidden, is very subtle. It may hide behind an illusion, in neuroticism, in make-believe, in some family name. Uncover every stone, every blade of grass, to find out.

Either you take time to find out, which becomes a bondage, or you see the thing, grasp it, have an insight into it instantly. When you have a complete insight it covers the whole field.

How can the brain, which is conditioned, grasp the unlimited, which is beauty, love, and truth? What is the ground of compassion and intelligence, and can it come upon each one of us? Are you inviting compassion? Are you inviting intelligence? Are you inviting beauty, love, and truth?

Are you trying to grasp it? I am asking you. Are you trying to grasp the quality of intelligence, compassion, the immense sense of beauty, the perfume of love, and that truth that has no path to it? Is that what you are grasping, wanting to find out the ground upon which it dwells? Can the limited brain grasp this?

You cannot possibly grasp it, hold it, though you do all kinds of meditation, fast, torture yourself, become terribly austere, have only one piece of clothing. The rich cannot come to the truth, neither can the poor, nor the people who have taken a vow of celibacy, of silence, of austerity. All that is determined by thought, put together sequentially by thought; it is all the cultivation of deliberate thought, of deliberate intent. As the brain is limited, do whatever you will; sit cross-legged in the lotus posture, go off into a trance, meditate, stand on your head, or on one leg—whatever you do, you will never come upon it; compassion does not come.

Therefore one must understand what love is. Love is not sensation. Love is not pleasure, desire, fulfilment. Love is not jealousy, hatred. Love has sympathy, generosity, and tact, but these qualities are not love. To understand that, to come to that, requires a great sense and appreciation of beauty. Not the beauty of a woman or of a man, or a cinema star. Beauty is not in the mountain, in the skies, in the valleys, or in the flowing river. Beauty exists only where there is love. And beauty, love, is compassion.

There is no ground for compassion; it does not stay at your convenience. That beauty, love, truth, is the highest form of intelligence. When there is that intelligence, there is action, clarity, a tremendous sense of dignity. It is something unimaginable. And that which is not to be imagined, or the unlimited, cannot be put into words. It can be described; philosophers have described it, but the philosophers who have described it are not that which they have described.

To come upon this great sense, there must be the absence of the "me," the ego, egocentric activity, the becoming. There must be a great silence in one. Silence means emptiness of everything. In that there is vast space. Where there is vast space there is immense energy—not self-interested energy, but unlimited energy.

Death is the most extraordinary thing, putting an end to long continuity. In that continuity we hope to find security, because the brain can only function excellently when it is completely secure—secure from terrorism, secure in a belief, secure in knowledge, and so on. All that comes to an end when there is death. I may have hope for a next life and all that stuff, but death is really the ending of a long continuity. I have identified myself with that continuity. That continuity is "me." And death says, "Sorry, old boy, that is the end." And you are not frightened of death, really not frightened, if you are living constantly with death, that is, constantly ending. Not continuing and ending, but ending every day that which you have gathered, that which you have memorized, that which you have experienced.

Time gives us hope, thought gives us comfort, thought assures us a continuity, and we say, "Well, in the next life …"But if I do not end this silliness now, the stupidity, the illusions, they would be there in a next life, if there were a next life. Time, thought, give continuity, and we cling to that continuity, and therefore there is fear. And fear destroys love. Love, compassion, and death are not separate movements.

Can we live with death, and can thought and time have a stop? They are all related. Do not separate time, thought, and death. It is all one thing.

[5]

THREE ARTS IN OUR DAILY LIFE

I THINK we ought to understand very clearly and simply the art of listening, the art of seeing, and the art of learning. The word *art* is generally applied to artists, those who paint, those who write poems, make sculpture, and so on. But the meaning of that word *art* is giving everything its right place, putting all our thoughts, feelings, anxieties, and so on, in their right place, giving the proper proportion to things, putting everything in harmony.

We rarely listen to anybody. We are so full of our own conclusions, our own experiences, our own problems, our own judgments, that we have no space in which to listen. To listen is possible only when you put aside your particular opinion, your particular knowledge or problem, your conclusions. Then you are free to listen without interpreting, judging, evaluating. Actually, the art of listening is to listen with great care, with attention, with affection. If you are capable of such listening, then communication becomes very simple. There will be no misunderstanding. Communication implies to think together, to share the things that we are talking about together, to partake in the problem as two human beings. Living in a monstrous, corrupt world where everything is so ugly, brutal, violent, and meaningless, communication seems very important to me. In the art of listening one learns immediately, one sees the fact instantly. In the art of listening there is freedom, and in that freedom every nuance of a word has significance and there is immediate comprehension. There is immediate insight and therefore immediate freedom to observe.

There is also the art of seeing, to see things as they are, not as you wish to see them; to see things without any illusion, without any preconceived judgment or opinion, to see what actually is, not your conclusions about what is.

Then, there is the art of learning. Not memorizing, which becomes very mechanical. Our brains have already become extraordinarily mechanical. The art of learning implies freedom to observe, to listen without prejudice, without argumentation, without any emotional, romantic responses.

If we actually, not intellectually, have these three arts in our daily life, putting everything in its right place, where it belongs, then we can live a really very quiet, harmonious life. So please learn now the art of listening. See with the attention of listening that thought is time, thought is measure, thought is a movement in time, which creates fear. If you do not make a conclusion of that statement, but actually listen with your heart, with your mind, with all your capacity, attention, and care, then you will see that fear has no place at all. The art of listening is the miracle.

So listen, not thinking what to do about it. The art of listening is to be sensitive, to be alert, to be watchful, *now*. If you are doing that now, you will see that you will put thought in its right place. Then you will have an actual relationship with another, and therefore never have conflict with another.

Our consciousness is our daily, everyday life. In that consciousness there is the desire for power, the many hurts that one has received from childhood. There is fear, pleasure, and the thing that we call *love*, which is not love. There are the innumerable beliefs that we have—belief in God or belief in no god, belief in socialism, belief in capitalism. Belief indicates a life that is based on make-believe, which has nothing to do with actuality.

We are bringing order in consciousness, not by wanting order, not by making an effort to bring about order, but by listening, seeing, learning. To listen there must be no direction. To see there must be no distortion. And to learn, not to memorize, there must be freedom to observe and to watch.

[6]

LAYING THE FOUNDATION OF MEDITATION

I WONDER often why we come together, listening to a speaker, half serious, curious, and not really wanting to change our life totally. We become rather mediocre, without a flair, without any quality of genius. I am using *genius* in the sense, not of any particular talent or particular gift, but of a mind that comprehends the totality of life, which is a vast, complex, contradictory, unhappy existence. One listens, and one goes away with partial understanding, with no deep intention and serious attention to bring about a deep psychological revolution. I wonder often why human beings tolerate the kind of lives they lead. You may blame the circumstances, the society, the political organization, but blaming others has not solved our problems. We drift and life seems such a waste, going to an office from morning till night for fifty years or so and then retiring to die or vegetate or grumble or fade away quietly.

When one looks at one's own life with all its extraordinary beauty, the vastness of what we have achieved technologically, one wonders why there has been so little beauty in our life. I mean by that word not merely the appearance of beauty, the decoration of the outer, but that quality of great communication with nature. If one loses contact with nature, one loses relationship with other human beings. You may read poems if you are so inclined, you may read all the beautiful sonnets and hear the lyrical swing of a lovely poem, but imagination is not beauty. The appreciation of a cloud and the love of light in that cloud, and of a sheet of water along a dry road, or a bird perched on a single branch—all that enchantment we rarely see or appreciate or love because we are occupied with our own problems, with our own worries, with our peculiar ideas and fixations, and are never free. Beauty is this quality of freedom that is totally different from independence.

When you hear all this, I wonder what you make of it. When we do not see a dog and love that dog, or a rock, or a stray cloud passing by, when we have not that sense of extraordinary communication with the world that brings about great beauty, we become small human beings, mediocre, wasting our extraordinary life and losing all the beauty and the depth of existence. We must get back to realities, but that is also real, extraordinarily real. The branch, the shadow, the light on a leaf, the fluttering parrot, is also actual, real, and when we understand the swaying palm tree and the whole feeling of life, then there is a great sense of depth to beauty. But I am afraid we are not interested in that. We listen, and let it slip by. It may sound romantic, sentimental, but beauty is not romantic, not sentimental, nor emotional. It is something very, very solid, like a rock in the midst of a fast-flowing stream.

We must investigate order, because our life is disorderly, confused, contradictory. We are talking very simply. Where there is contradiction, there is no order. Where there is confusion, conflict, there is no order; and our life, as we live it daily, is a mass of contradiction, confusion, conflict, and dishonesty. That is a fact. And one wonders if order can be brought about in this confusion, because without order there is no efficiency. Order has nothing whatever to do with sentiment, with romance. Order is sequential, logical, sane.

So, can we have order—not a blueprint, not something laid down by tradition or by a guru or by a leader or by our own little desires and compulsions—but lasting order? How can we bring about order in our lives so that there is no opposite, duality, contradiction, dishonesty, whether politically, religiously, or in our relationship with each other? We can go often into some kind of illusion and think that we are meditating, but without bringing about order in our daily life, do what we will, there can be no meditation. So we are laying the foundation of meditation.

The first thing is to realize how disorderly our daily life is, to be aware. It is not how to bring order in disorder, but to understand the nature of disorder. When I understand the nature of disorder, then out of that comprehension, out of that obvious fact, comes the beauty of order that is not imposed or disciplined or suppressed or from conformity. Out of the very investigating of disorder, order comes naturally. Now, let's do it.

Human beings have extraordinary capacity. Technologically, immense things have been done. Human beings are extraordinarily capable, have thought out almost every form of concepts, principles, ideas, religious projections; they have invented rituals, some of which are really most beautiful, but they have no meaning at all. The human mind has great qualities. The mind is not only the various forms of sensory activities, but is the emotions, affection, care, attention, the intellectual capacity, and that sense of great love. All that is the mind, the wholeness of the mind. Will you challenge that as we are talking, so that it shall operate at its highest, greatest excellence? Because if you do not challenge it, you live in disorder.

We are asking why human beings, for centuries upon centuries, have accepted living in disorder, politically, religiously, economically, socially, and in our relationship with each other. Why? Why have we accepted living this way?

From whom do you expect the answer? A challenge implies that you respond with your highest capacity. I have challenged your mind. The speaker has said: exercise your highest capacity, exercise all your energy to find out whether it is possible to live in a world that is degenerating, corrupt, immoral, whether you can live a sane life that is completely whole. That is your challenge. What is your response to it? The word *whole* means healthy, both physically and psychologically, with all the capacities of your mind; that is sanity. And the word *whole* also means holy, sacred. That is the whole of life.

Are you as a human being aware of the total disorder and the degenerating process going on in the world around you and in yourself? Aware in the sense of observing what is actually taking place. Not imagining what is taking place, not making an idea of what is taking place, but the actual happening: the political, the religious, the social, the moral degeneration of man. No institution, no guru, no higher principles, are going to stop this degradation. It is happening the world over. Are we aware of that? If we are, then what shall we do? What is our action? Not at some future date— what is our *immediate* action? Will we escape from the actual fact of the brain that is getting old, degenerating, or will we, together, investigate, explore, why human beings have become like this?

What shall we do? I would suggest that we first look at our life, at what it actually is, at what is happening in our life, because our life in action is society. Our life in action is our society, and you cannot transform that society unless you transform yourself. That is so obvious. The communist, the liberal, the socialist will not alter it. Reading the Gita or the Upanishads will not alter it, or becoming terribly interested in what Buddhism has to say, or following Zen meditation. None of those will solve it. So let us look at what is happening in our life, our daily life.

Our daily life is based on relationship. Without relationship you cannot possibly exist. What is your relationship with others, with your wife, with your husband, with your boss, with your factory worker, with your neighbor? What is the relationship with each other? In that relationship, is there order, or self-centered activity opposed to another self-centered activity? That is contradiction. I may be married, have children, sex, and all the rest of it, and if I am self-centered, concerned about my own success, my ambition, my status, worrying about myself, and my wife is also concerned about herself, her problems, her beauty, her looks, how can there be any kind of relationship between the two people? If you have one belief and another has another kind of belief or another kind of conclusion, another kind of dogma, there is no relationship. Haven't you noticed all this? So, is it possible to bring order in your relationship, with your wife and husband, not with the universe, not with cosmos, not with "God"? God is an invention of the intellect. You can have extraordinary relationship with those things that you have invented, deal with illusions, but to have relationship with your wife and husband and children so that there is no conflict, that is where order begins.

Now, how will you bring order there? Order is sequence in space—listen to the beauty of it. Space in the mind. That means a mind that is never occupied with any problem. But our minds are so occupied, so crowded with belief, with pursuit of all kinds of things, confusion, illusion, that there is no space. Where there is no space, there cannot be sequence and order. And if there is no order in our daily life, meditation is merely an escape from your life. And escape into meditation leads only to illusion.

So one must lay the foundation to find out that which is beyond thought, that which is immeasurable, that which has no word. But that cannot come into being without this sense of great order in which there is total freedom.

[7]

THE ART OF LIVING

MOST OF US are fragmented, broken up into business life, religious life, family life, sexual life, and so on. We are not holistic, whole human beings. We look at life from a particular point of view, from a conclusion, or from some idealistic concept. These are all a fragmented outlook on life. Can we face a problem from a wholly different outlook that is not fragmented at all? Recognizing, being aware that we are fragmented, broken up, divided in ourselves, contradictory, opposing one desire against another desire, is it possible that we could face a problem from a different focus?

Why do we have problems? We have multiple problems in life, and problems are increasing in a society that is so sophisticated, so complex, overpopulated, with bad governments, and so on. In the resolution of one problem we seem to increase many other problems. Why do we have problems, and is it possible to meet a problem without a brain that is already conditioned to solve problems?

Let's look at it. We go to school very young, age five or seven, and as children we are faced with problems: how to write, how to read, how to learn mathematics. So from childhood our brain is conditioned to solving problems. One goes to college where there are again problems; then university, jobs, various functions, vocations, and so on, problem after problem. Our brain is full of problems. And we are always seeking solutions from a brain that is conditioned to solve problems. Now, how can the brain solve problems if it is not free from problems?

Our brains are conditioned from childhood to the resolution of problems. Because the brain is conditioned to solve problems, it is always seeking a solution. It is not understanding the problem itself but seeking the solution of the problem. Is it possible to have a brain that is not conditioned to problems?

Our brain is conditioned now to the solution of problems, and we have never solved the problems. They are increasing more and more. Why? Is it because a conditioned brain, which is embedded in problems, can never solve problems? Is it possible to have a brain that is not conditioned to the solution of problems and so can understand problems? Isn't there a difference between the solving of a problem and the understanding of a problem? In the understanding of a problem, the solution may lie in the problem.

Take a very ordinary example. We have never stopped wars. Human beings have had wars since they came on this earth. We have never solved the problem of war. We decided to reorganize how to kill man better—and this is called progress. This is not a joke. We move from organization to organization. First we had the League of Nations, and now we have the United Nations, but wars go on. We move from one organization to another, hoping thereby to solve problems. And we multiply problems and never stop wars.

The cause of wars is nationalism, economic division, local division. Linguistic, racial, religious, economic, and cultural divisions divide us. We are all human beings, we all suffer, we all have pain and anxiety, boredom, loneliness, despair. We do not tackle that, but we want to solve the problems that seem to have external causes.

Can the brain, recognizing, seeing that it from childhood, be free of the conditioning and then face problems? Will you do it? That is the question. Can we be conscious, be aware that our brain, that we as human beings, from the beginning of life, are always struggling with problems and trying to find the right answer to them? The right answer can be only when we recognize that the brain is conditioned and that as long as that brain is conditioned to solving problems we will never find the right answer.

If one cannot get on with one's wife, one divorces, then chooses another person, and keeps on repeating this. If one has plenty of time and energy this is the game that is going on in the world, on a smaller or bigger scale. But the problem is not divorce and all the complications of relationship, but to understand the depth of relationship, the meaning of relationship. Relationship, as we pointed out, is one of the most important things in life; not the emotional expressions of it, the tantrums, the neuroticism of relationship, but depth in relationship. And we never ask about that. We want to solve the problem of relationship—and so we never solve it. The psychiatrists, psychotherapists, and so on, are multiplying in the world like mushrooms. And they are not solving problems. They are not solving the depth of all this.

We should consider together the art of living. What is the art of living? We have the art of poetry, painting, the art of cooking, and so on. But we have never asked ourselves what the art of living is, which is, perhaps, the greatest art. Is there an art, or is it all just chance, some genetic, biological chance? If you make a problem of it, then the art is thrown out of the window.

So, let's look together to find out what the art of living is, using art with the width and the depth of that word, not just as the contents of a museum. If you were asked what the art of living is, what would your answer be? A calculated answer, personal answer, or emotional or romantic answer is meaningless. Right? If I answer that question emotionally—oh, the art of living is the highest aspiration, or the art of living is the most exalted intellectual activity—it is sheer nonsense; that is only very partial. Or to say that the art of living is to have a holistic outlook on life—it sounds excellent but factually it is not. So what is the art of living? Obviously, it is to have no conflict whatsoever. A brain that is in conflict all the time, that has problems all the time, tremendous self-concern, such a brain must inevitably be limited. If one is thinking about oneself, for example, how to meditate or whether you can, your very meditation is self-centeredness. You can add more to it, but it appears that the art of living is to live without conflict.

Is that possible at all? That is, to understand the opposing elements in one's life, desiring one thing, and opposing that with another desire. You know this corridor of dualities. As long as self-centeredness exists, there must be conflict, because self-centeredness is limited, small, petty. You hear all this but you carry on. You say that it is not possible in modern society to live without self-centeredness—at least a little bit of it. Have you ever tried? Have you ever lived without self-centeredness for one day, not thinking about yourself? Even just for an hour! And see what happens. You haven't committed to anything! You can go back to your self-centeredness, nobody is going to say how wrong it is, or how right it is; that is the normal state of human beings, apparently. So, really try for an hour actually to do it—not try it, do it—and see what happens. And if you do it for one hour you can extend it. And it gives you tremendous energy. It gives you a great sense of passion, not lust and all that, but passion to pursue something profoundly to the very end.

What is attention? Is it a physical act? Is it the movement of thought? Is it an action of desire, which is the essence of will? How does attention come about? Can it come naturally, easily, without making tremendous effort, without going to college, or attending some guru, being trained? We are going to look at the question, not the answer.

Attention implies not only the hearing of the ear but hearing without the ear. Attention also implies seeing, perceiving; seeing visually, but also seeing with the inner eye, as it were. Attention also means learning. Seeing, hearing, and learning. Those three things are implied.

What is learning? Is it memorizing as we do when we go to school, college, university, memorizing, storing up knowledge from books, from professors, from teachers, from housemasters, and so on and so on? That is always accumulating knowledge and using that knowledge, skillfully or not. An apprentice to a master carpenter is learning the nature of the wood, the kinds of wood, the grain, the beauty of the wood, the feeling of the wood, and the instruments that he is employing. He is learning; and that learning is through experience, day after day, month after month, accumulating knowledge about carpentry. That is what we call learning. That kind of learning is limited, obviously, because all knowledge is limited, now or in the past or in the future.

Is there a learning that is not limited? Is there a learning that is not an accumulative process of learning knowledge, but in which is implied hearing not only the words, the significance of the words, your reactions to the words, your responses to certain favorite words, like *love* and *hate*, but also seeing without any prejudice, seeing without the word? Can you look at a tree without the word? Have you ever done this? That means seeing without direction, without motive, without any network of thought blocking the seeing. Learning is a limitless process.

Attention implies all that. And the beginning of it is to be aware. Are we aware of our surroundings as we sit here, looking at it all without a single word? To be aware. But in awareness you begin to choose—I like that blue shirt better than what I am wearing. I like the way your hair is done, better than mine. You are always comparing, judging, evaluating, which is choice. Can we be aware without choice?

Will you do it? If we are doing this, then we begin to discover that awareness is entirely different from concentration. Concentration implies focusing all thought on a particular subject, on a particular page, on a particular word. Which implies cutting off all other thoughts, building resistance to every other thought, which then becomes narrow, limited. So concentration is limited. But you have to concentrate when you are doing something. When you are washing dishes, you have to wash them very carefully, use the right kind of soap, the right kind of water. You know all this. Awareness without choice, which means without concentration, is to be aware without judging, evaluating, condemning, comparing, and from that, move. That is attention, which is natural.

When I want to listen to a story you are telling me, a very exciting thriller, I listen to you very carefully. When you are telling me something very, very serious, I am so eager, so attentive to understand what you are saying that I pay attention. I understand what I am thinking about, that is irrelevant, but I am tremendously concerned with what you are saying. Therefore I am all attention; all my nerves, my whole being, wants to understand what you are talking about.

In that attention there is no "me." Get it? When there is this tremendous attention, which means when all my energy is given to understand, I am not thinking about myself. Therefore there is no center in me that says "I must attend."

[8]

BE COMPLETELY FREE OF FEAR

I AM GOING to investigate something totally new, and I hope you will have the kindness and the seriousness to listen, not agreeing or disagreeing but thinking together logically, sanely, rationally, and with a certain sense of humility.

Skill becomes all important in life, because that is the means of earning a livelihood. Our universities, colleges, and schools are directed for that purpose. When one is totally educated for that purpose, that skill invariably breeds a certain sense of power, arrogance, and self-importance. What is the relationship of skill to clarity? And what is the relationship of clarity to compassion?

We have talked very often about the art of listening, the art of seeing, the art of learning. The art of listening is to listen so that naturally everything is put in its right place. The meaning of that word, art, is to put things where they belong. And the art of seeing is to observe without any distortion. Obviously. If there is any distortion there is no observation. To see clearly, to have great clarity in perception, there must be no distortion. Distortion is brought about by any form of motive, purpose, direction.

The art of learning is not only the accumulation of knowledge, which is necessary for skillful action, but also learning without accumulation. There are two types of learning. There is acquiring and gathering knowledge through experience, through books, through education; the brain is registering, accumulating knowledge, storing it up, and acts from that storage of knowledge, skillfully or unskillfully. Another form of learning is never to accumulate, is to become so totally aware that you only register what is absolutely necessary and nothing else. Then the mind is not cluttered up all the time with the movement of knowledge.

So, there are three essential things in the awakening of intelligence. There is the art of listening without distortion, and to communicate not only verbally but nonverbally exactly what you mean. The art of seeing is to observe clearly without a direction, without motive, without any form of desire, merely to observe. And the art of learning, accumulating knowledge, means registering all the things that are necessary for skillful action, and not registering any psychological responses, any psychological reactions, so that the brain is employing itself only where function and skill are necessary.

It is very arduous to be so totally aware that you register only what is necessary and absolutely do not register anything that is not necessary. Someone insults you, someone flatters you, someone calls you this or that, and there is no registration. It gives tremendous clarity to register what is necessary and not to register what is not necessary, so there is no psychological building up of the "me," the structure of the self. The structure of the self arises only when there is registration of everything that is not necessary. That is, giving importance to one's name, form, one's experience, one's opinions, conclusions; all that is the gathering up of the energy of the self, which is always distorting.

Listening without any conclusion, without any opinion, which are distorting factors, one discovers the false and the true without any effort, because when there is actual attention given to listening, that very attention excludes everything that is not absolutely factual. When you observe with conclusions, opinions, dogmas, beliefs, you cannot possibly see very clearly. Learning to act skillfully in life is necessary, but any other form of registering distorts, gives importance to skill and therefore becomes mechanical.

The art of listening, the art of seeing, the art of learning give extraordinary clarity, and that clarity can communicate verbally. If there is no clarity, skill in action breeds self-importance, whether that self-importance is identified with a group or with oneself, or with a nation. And that self-importance denies clarity, naturally. You cannot have clarity without compassion. Because we have no compassion, skill has become more important.

Clarity is denied when there is any form of fear. Most human beings have a great deal of fear—which denies compassion. Fear in any form, both physiological as well as psychological, distorts clarity; therefore, a person who is afraid in any way has no compassion. There are various forms of fear—of growing old, of losing your husband, wife, child, fear of not being successful. You do not have to invite fear; it is there. So you can look at the fear now, because you are a living human being now and in that state your fears, though they may be dormant, are still there consciously or unconsciously.

The art of seeing, the art of observing very clearly, is possible only when you do not want to get rid of fear, because then that becomes a distorting factor. If you are unconscious of your fears, that is also a distorting factor. The many fears have a common root. It is like a tree that has many branches and leaves. Fear also has many branches, many leaves, many expressions of fear that breed their own flowering and their own fruit, which is action. So one must go to the very root of fear, not take various forms of fears but the root of fear.

Look: one may be afraid of darkness, one may be afraid of losing one's wife or husband, one may be afraid of having no money, one may be afraid of some past pain and not want it again, one may be afraid of a dozen things. One can go through them analytically one by one—and that is such a waste of time, isn't it? Whereas it would be much simpler and more direct if you go to the root of fear.

I think many of us do not realize or are aware deeply of the nature of fear and what it does to human beings. When there is fear, there are many kinds of neurotic action. Most of you are lonely, and so you seek companionship, escaping from loneliness. Companionship becomes very important, and if you have no companionship fear arises. Or out of that loneliness you build a wall around yourself; you resist, you escape, and out of that escape, resistance, suppression, grows every form of neurotic action. So it is very important to understand the nature and the structure of fear, because it will not give clarity. And if there is no clarity there is no awakening of intelligence, which is neither yours nor mine. That intelligence has its own action, which is non mechanistic, and therefore without cause.

So it is very important to understand fear and be completely free of it. Do we see the importance and the urgency of wiping fear away, conscious fear and fears of which we are not conscious? One can deal with conscious fears comparatively easily, but it is much more difficult to be free of fears of which you do not know, fears that are hidden. How are you going to examine the deep-rooted fears? Is it possible to examine them? Psychologists say it is possible through analysis, through dreams, through careful psychoanalytical therapy. Analysis does not clear up the mind. There is no clarity in analysis because the more you analyze, the more there is to analyze. And it might take you the whole of your life; at the end of it you have nothing!

We are going to think together to find out the truth of analysis, the truth, not yours or mine. First of all, in analysis there is the observer and the observed, the analyzer and the analyzed. The analyzer says, "I am going to analyze my reactions, my dreams, my desires, my fears." But is the analyzer different from the fear, different from what he is going to analyze? You must be very clear on this. Is the analyzer different from the analyzed? If you say they are different, which most people do, then you are caught in everlasting conflict. That is, when the analyzer examines his responses—jealousy, anger, violence—in that examination, in that analysis, the examiner thinks he is separate. And this separation will inevitably divide, and therefore there must be conflict. Where there is division, there must be conflict, whether the division is between two nations or between man and woman. Not that the woman is the same as the man; obviously, biologically they are not. But the ideas, the accumulated responses of each, the images they have of each other, divide, and therefore there is conflict in relationships.

So, when there is analysis, there must inevitably be conflict. Most unfortunately, we are educated to have conflict. It is the way of our life; if we have no conflict we say, "What is wrong with me?" And to have conflict is the essence of neuroticism.

And in analysis time is necessary. It might take days, months, years; if you have the energy, the capacity, the money, then you can go on analyzing yourself endlessly. It becomes quite fun! Then you have somebody to go to, to tell them all about your troubles and pay whatever you pay. That is such a waste of time. It is postponement of the immediate solution of the problem. Analysis implies conflict, analysis implies time, analysis implies no ending to any problem. That is a fact. So when you see the truth of this, or see the fact, you will never analyze.

Then what will you do? Psychologically, analysis not only breeds time, division, but also each analysis must be complete, mustn't it? Otherwise the incompleteness of analysis is brought over from yesterday, and with the incomplete analysis you examine the new fact. So there is always a coloring of the present from the past. If you see this very clearly, and I hope you do, then what will you do if you do not analyze? If you see analysis is a false process, if you yourself actually see the truth that analysis does not lead anywhere, then what will you do?

Now we are going to take fear. Most of us are accustomed to analyze fear, its cause and the effect. What has made one afraid? One seeks the cause. That is a process of analysis. It may be a hundred causes, or it may be a single cause. And the effect becomes the cause for the next fear. So there is causation, effect, and the effect becomes the cause. So when you are seeking a cause you are caught up in this chain, and therefore there is no release from this chain. This is part of analysis.

So one asks, "If there is no analysis, then what will happen to my fear?" There may be a dozen fears but we are concerned with the root, not with the branches. If you can pull out the root it is finished, the whole tree is dead. So, what is the root of fear? Is it time? One form of time is chronological, time by the watch, twenty-four hours, sunset to sunrise. There is another form of time that is psychological time. That is the "tomorrow." Psychologically, 1 will solve my problems the day after tomorrow. So is fear the result of time? I have had pain yesterday or last week, and that pain is registered in the brain. And when that pain is registered, then there is fear of that pain happening again a week later. When there is no registration of the pain, then there is no fear.

There is fear when there is measurement. When one measures oneself against somebody else, there is fear. I am not as intelligent as you are, and I would like to be as intelligent as you are, and I am afraid I may not be. All that is a movement of time, which is measurement, which is comparison. So measurement, time, comparison, imitation breed fear. And that time, measurement, comparison, is the movement of thought. So thought is the very root of fear. Please see the logic, the reasoning of this.

We are thinking together, examining together, taking the journey together to find out. And we see analysis is not the solution; finding the cause is not the solution; and time is not the solution, time being measurement, comparison. Time is the movement of thought. So the problem then is not how to be free of fear, or how to suppress fear, but to understand the whole movement of thought. See how far we have gone away from the demand to be free of fear? We are entering into something much greater, much more comprehensive. If there is understanding of the whole movement of thought, it must be holistic, whole. And fear arises only when there is the "me," which is the small, not the whole.

In the art of learning, the art of seeing, the art of listening, there is no movement of thought. If I am just listening to you, why should I interfere with my thoughts? I am seeing, observing; in that observation there is no movement of thought. I just observe. I observe the mountain, the tree, the river, the people, without any projection of my background and so on, which is the movement of thought. Thought is necessary to accumulate knowledge to function skillfully, but otherwise thought has no place whatsoever. And this brings tremendous clarity, doesn't it?

I hope you have clarity. Clarity means there is no center from which you are functioning, no center put together by thought as the "me," "mine," "they" and "we." Where there is a center, there must be a circumference, and where there is a circumference, there is resistance, there is division, and that is one of the fundamental "causes" of fear—*causes* in quotes.

So when we consider fear, we are considering the whole movement of thought, which breeds fear. And clarity is possible only when thought is completely in abeyance; that is, when thought has its right place, which is to act in the field of knowledge and not enter into any other field. In that, there is total elimination of all opinion, judgment, evaluation. There is only listening, seeing, and learning. Without clarity, skill becomes a most destructive thing in life, which is what is happening in the world. You can go to the moon and put the flag of your country up there, which is not clarity. You can kill each other through wars, by the extraordinary development of technology, which is the movement of thought. You can divide yourselves into races, communes, and so on and so on, which are all divisions created by thought.

Thought is a fragment. Thought is limited. Thought is conditioned. Thought is narrow, because thought is based on experience, memory, knowledge, which is the past, which is time-binding. That which is time-binding is necessarily limited, therefore thought is limited. So thought can never understand that which is whole. Thought can never understand that which is immeasurable, which is timeless. One can imagine the timeless, the immeasurable; thought can put up all kinds of imaginary future structures. But it is still limited. So, "God" put together by thought is limited. I am afraid those of you who believe in God won't see this, because your God is the result of your thought, of your fears, of your desire to be secure.

Please see the truth of this, and clarity will come like sun out of the clouds. See that thought is the word, and that the word is never the thing. The word is the description of the thing, but the thing is not the description. Fear then becomes completely useless, it has no meaning. Then you have to find out whether thought can ever remain in its field and not move out of that field to register.

It is the function of the brain to register so that it can be secure, so that it can be safe. It is safe, secure in the field of knowledge. You cannot live without security. One must have food, clothing, and shelter, not for the few but for the whole. And that is only possible when thought only operates in that field and when it does not register in any other direction. Then there is no nationality, there is no "you" and "me." There is no division, because when there is no registration the mind is free to look, the mind is free to observe.

When there is that clarity, skill never becomes mechanical, because whatever the skill may be, it is functioning, acting from that clarity that is born out of compassion. One has to inquire very deeply into what compassion is. We have talked very clearly about clarity and skill, and the dangers of skill without clarity. There are three things, which are compassion, clarity, and skill. And when there is compassion, there is no division between clarity and skill, it is one movement. Because we are caught up in skill, we do not see the total movement.

What is the nature and the structure of compassion? To understand it, one must go into pleasure, love, suffering, death. You cannot just say, "I have compassion." The mind that says "I am compassionate" is not compassionate. When the mind says, "I am intelligent," it is no longer intelligent because it is conscious of itself; when it is conscious of itself there is no intelligence.

To go into the depth and the meaning and the significance and the beauty of compassion, we must inquire not only, as we did, into fear, but also into pleasure. Is love pleasure? Is love desire? Is love of another a remembrance? Is love of another an image? All these are involved when we think over together this matter of compassion. And we can go into it only when we go together. Because a human being is not alone, one human being is the essence of all human beings. That is a fact; that is a reality. It is not my invention, my wanting to identify myself with the whole.

The absolute fact is that you, as a human being, living through millennia after millennia, are the representative of the whole of humanity that has suffered, agonized, shed tears, killed and been killed, that is jealous, angry, anxious, seeking pleasure, caught in fear. You are all that. Therefore you are the entire humanity. And when there is a total revolution in this consciousness, that revolution affects the consciousness of humanity. That is a fact. And that is why it is so urgently important that each one of us listens, is good enough to listen, is serious enough to take the journey together. When you fundamentally, deeply do that, when consciousness changes its content, you affect the whole of humanity.

[9]

ALL THE SENSES HIGHLY AWAKENED

WHAT IS BEAUTY? Is beauty according to a principle, according to certain rules? Or, though there must be attention to proportion and so on, is beauty something entirely different? When you see mountains, range after range, blue in the evening, and when the sun touches them in early morning before everything else, the reaction to that seeing is great silence. You keep quiet; there is space, enormous space, between you and that—and beyond. When you see such marvelous beautiful mountains, snow-clad against the blue sky, for an instant you become silent. The very beauty, the very grandeur, the majesty of the mountains keeps you, makes you absolutely quiet. You can say, the shock of beauty. When you see something extraordinarily grand, of great height and depth, then the very shock of that beauty drives away for the moment all your problems. There is no self wondering, worrying, talking to itself; there is no entity, the self, the "me," looking. At that moment when the self is not, there is great beauty.

What is the role of art in our lives? Why should anything play a role in our lives? The greatest art is the art of living, not the paintings, the sculpture, the poems, and the marvelous literature. They have their place, but to find out for oneself the art of living is the greatest art. It surpasses any role in life.

Aesthetics is the capacity of perception, the capacity to perceive, which means one must be extraordinarily sensitive; and sensitivity comes from the depth of silence. It is no good going to colleges and universities to learn how to be sensitive, or to go to somebody to teach you how to be sensitive. You cannot perceive if there is not a certain depth of silence. If you look at trees in silence, there is a communication that is "not merely verbal, but a communication, a communion with nature. Most of us have lost our relationship with nature: with the trees, with the mountain, with all the living things of the earth.

Sensitivity in our relationship is to be aware of each other. Is that at all possible? The art of living is to find a relationship that is not conflict, that is a flow of a harmonious manner of living together without all the quarrels, possessiveness and being possessed, and fear of loneliness—the whole cycle of human struggle. The art of living is far more important than the art of great painters. Listening to music, going into all the museums of the world and talking about them endlessly, reading books on art, all that may be an escape from our own troubles, anxieties, depressions.

Can we live an aesthetic life of deep perception, be aware of our words, be aware of noise, of the vulgarity of human beings? One learns far more in silence than in noise. These may sound like platitudes, but they are not. This requires a great deal of observation of oneself. That observation is prevented by any form of authority, looking to another to teach us how to observe. Just observe, watch the way we walk, the way we talk, the noise that goes on. Then out of that comes the art of living.

Art, as we said, is putting things together harmoniously. It is to observe the contradictions in oneself, one's desires that are always so strong, to observe all that, not create an opposite of it, just to observe the fact and live with the fact. It seems that is the way to bring about a life of harmony.

I hope you look at mountains, not at me. The speaker is not important at all. What he says may be important or may not be important, but you have to discover for yourself.

What is important in life? What is the root or the basic essential in life? As one observes more and more in television, and literature, magazines, and all the things that are going on, answers are becoming more and more superficial, quick. If you are in trouble, you go to specialists, and they tell you what to do. It is all becoming so superficial and vulgar—if one may use that word without any sense of being derogatory or insulting. It is all becoming rather childish.

One never asks what the fundamental questions are or what the fundamental necessity is for the depth of life. Surely it is not beliefs, dogmas, faith, not all the intellectual rigmarole, whether in the communist ideology or the Catholic theology, Marx or Lenin, or Saint Thomas Aquinas. They are all the same: theories, conclusions, and ideologies, based on belief, faith, dogma, rituals. So all that is becoming more and more superficial outwardly in one's life. And we live like that. This is a fact, I am not saying anything that is not so.

We have the marvelous worlds of entertainment, religion, and football—

anything to escape. Yell, shout, never a quiet conversation, never looking at anything quietly, beautifully. So what is the fundamental, basic demand or basic thing that is really of the utmost importance in one's life?

Can thought be aware of itself? Thought has created the thinker separate from his thought. There is the thinker who says, "I must be aware of what I think, I must control my thoughts, I must not let my thoughts wander." And the thinker acts upon the thought. Now, is the thinker different from thought? Or has the thinking, thought, created the thinker? There is no thinker without thought.

Please, it is rather important to find out why this duality exists in us, the opposites, the contradiction: the "me" and the thought, the "me" as the thinker, the one who witnesses, the one who observes, and the thing to be observed. That is, the thinker then controls thought, shapes thought, puts thought into a mold. But is the thinker different from thought? Has not thought created the thinker?

Let us be logical. Verbally, intellectually, I can see very clearly that there is the division between the thinker and the thought, and that thought has created the thinker. So the thinker is the past, with his memories, with his knowledge, all put together by thought, which has come into being after experiences. So the thinker is the whole activity of the past. And then it says, "Thinking is something different from me, the thinker." We accept that logically, intellectually, very quickly. But why? Why do we say that we understand it intellectually? Why is the first reaction to say, "I understand intellectually"? Is it not because we never look at the whole thing? We only look at something intellectually. Why does one do that? Is it that the intellect is highly developed with most of us, or developed much more than our sensitivity, our immediate perception? Of course. Because we are trained from childhood to acquire, to memorize, to exercise certain parts of the brain to hold what it has been told, and keep on repeating it. So when we meet something new, we say, "I understand intellectually." We never meet the new totally, wholly, that is with all our senses awakened. We never receive it completely; we receive it partially, and the partial activity is the intellectual activity. It is never the whole being observing. We say, "Yes, that is logical," and we stop there. We do not ask why it is that only part of the senses are awakened.

Intellectual perception is partial sensitivity, partial senses acting. In creating a computer you think intellectually, you do not have to have all your emotions and your senses. You have become mechanical, and repeat that. The same process is carried over when we hear something new. We understand intellectually, we do not meet it entirely. A statement is made but we do not receive it totally.

Why is it that we never meet anything—especially when we see a tree or the mountains, or the movement of the sea—with all our senses highly awakened? Isn't it that we live always partially, that we live in a limited sphere, a limited space in ourselves? It is a fact.

So to look, look with all your senses. When that takes place, when you look with all your senses, your eyes, your ears, your nerves, the whole response of the organism, which is also the brain, there is no center as the "me" who is looking.

We are asking if thought can be aware of itself. That is rather a complex question, and requires very careful observation. Thought has created wars through nationalism, through sectarian religions. Thought has created all this; God has not created the hierarchy of the church—the pope, all the robes, all the rituals, the swinging of the incense, the candles. All that paraphernalia that goes on in a cathedral or in a church is put together by thought, copied, some of it, from the ancient Egyptians, from the ancient Hindus, and Hebrews. It is all thought. So "God" is created by thought.

Does a person who has no fear whatsoever of dying or of living, who is without problems, need "God"? One can see what thought has done, step by step. So thought can be aware of its own action, so that there is no contradiction between the thinker and the thought, between the observer and the observed. When there is no contradiction, there is no effort. It is only when there is contradiction, which is division, that there must be effort.

So to find out whether it is possible to live a life without a single shadow of effort, contradiction, one must investigate the whole movement of thought. And one has not the time or the inclination; one is too busy, has too much to do. But one has plenty of time when one wants to play golf.

To find out the activity of thought, to watch it, is part of meditation.

Have you ever inquired into what silence is? What is silence? What is peace? Is peace between two wars? That is what is happening. What we call peace is between two wars. This war, like the next war, is to end all wars. Is peace between two noises? Is peace between two wars? Is peace between two quarrels?

So what is silence? It cannot be bought in a shop or pharmacy. We would like to buy it quickly and get on with it. But silence or peace cannot be bought. If that is so, what is silence?

Silence must mean space, mustn't it? I can be very silent in a small space, enclose myself, shut my eyes, and put a wall round myself, concentrate on some petty little altair. and in that there can be a certain amount of peace, a certain amount of silence. I can go into my den, my reading room, or quiet room, and sit there; but the space is limited when I do that. Not only my little room, but in my brain also, the space is very, very limited. Because most of us have never even asked about, thought about all this.

So what is space? Is space from one point to another? Is space a limited dimension? Or is space without a center, and therefore without a border? As long as I have "me," my problems, my selfish demands, my, my, my, it is very limited. That limitation has its own small space. But that little space is a form of self-protective wall to remain within, not to be disturbed, not to have problems, not to have trouble, and so on. For most of us, that space of the self is the only space we have. And from that space we are asking what space is.

Where there is limitation, there cannot be vast space. That is all. And space implies silence. Noise does not imply space. With all the noise that is going on in towns, between people, and all the noise of modern music, there is no space. There is not silence anywhere, just noise. It may be pleasant or unpleasant, that is not the point.

So what does it mean to have space? The space between two notes on the piano is a very small space. Silence between two people who have been quarreling, and later on resume the quarreling, is a very limited space.

Is there a space that is limitless? Not in heaven, not in the universe, but in ourselves, in our whole way of living? To have space—not imagined, not romantic, but the actual feeling of a vast sense of space. Now, you will say, "Yes, I understand that intellectually." But receive that question entirely, with all your senses. Then you will find out if there is such a vast space—which is related to the universe.

Learning about oneself is infinite. Learning from books has certain limitations; all knowledge is limitation. There is no complete knowledge about anything. Even the scientists admit that. Outward knowledge is necessary and that same wave continues inwardly. The Greeks, and those before them, said "know yourself." That does not mean to go to somebody and find out about yourself. It means watch what you are doing, what you are thinking, your behavior, your words, your gestures, the way you talk, the way you eat. Watch! Not correct, not say this is right or wrong, just watch. And to watch there must be silence. In that watching there is learning; and when you are learning you become the teacher. So you are both the teacher and the disciple, and nobody else on earth. There is nobody outside who can free oneself, only one's own inward integrity, and having great humility so as to learn.

[10]

LOVE, FREEDOM, GOODNESS, BEAUTY ARE ONE

WE ARE talking about the art of living. I think we ought to go much more into it. Most of us have given very little thought to it; we have hardly inquired into the nature of what life is and how to live! our daily life with all its ugly turmoil, passing pleasures, and a great deal of entertainment, both religious and otherwise. We have studied academic subjects, spent years to become a doctor, a surgeon, or an engineer, and never at the end asked how to live a life without any conflict, without any of the problems that are involved in our daily unfortunate lives. We are always striving, reaching out, getting somewhere, and when a question, a challenge, is put before us, we say, "Yes, it sounds good, but tell me how to do it, what is the method, what is the system, so that we can live a life of great tranquillity, with a great sense of wonder, a sense of great beauty?"

I think we ought to banish "how" from our minds, not in the academic subjects, but in the psychological world. If one may most respectfully point out, never ask anybody how. They can only offer you a system, a method, which then becomes another bondage, another trap in which you are caught.

We have talked about wars. We have talked about how human beings are hurt psychologically from their childhood, hurt by their parents, by their schools, by their families. They are wounded people, and that wound inevitably breeds fear. We talked about fear a great deal. And we also talked about time, not only chronological time by the watch, but also time as a psychological means of achievement: "I am this, but I will be that," "I am violent, I will one day be nonviolent." This constant becoming from *what is* to what should be is also an element of time. Time is very important for us, not only physical time, to get from here to there, but also the ideal that thought has invented; to achieve an ideal also requires time. So we are bound to time. Writers and some other people have asked if there is an end to time, a stop to time.

Please kindly remember that we are investigating together deeply, seriously and with great honesty, how to live a life that is really a great art. So let's begin to inquire more. Humility is necessary to learn, isn't it? Humility, not humbleness, not a sense of remote acceptance; one needs a great deal of humility to learn. Most of us have not that quality of humility. It is not what you give to somebody whom you respect; that is not humility, that is merely acceptance of authority, and then you worship the authority.

Humility is necessary to understand the extraordinary complexity of living, humility with freedom. We think we are all very free to do what we want to do, to fulfil our desires. One of the structures of society is that each one of us is free to do exactly what he wants to do. You are all doing that. You want to be rich, you want to express yourself, you want to have your own particular way, you are very strong in your opinions, your conclusions. You are free to choose, and call this "freedom." Freedom has brought about great confusion, havoc in the world, each one expressing his own particular desire, competing.

What is freedom? Please ask this question of yourself. Is freedom a matter of choice? You are free to choose, free to go from here to there, free to have different kinds of jobs—if you don't like one you go to the other. You have freedom to express yourself, are free to think what you want and to express it, perhaps, in a democratic society. Not in totalitarian states—there freedom is denied.

So what is freedom? Does freedom really exist? Some of the root meaning of the word *freedom* is love. And is love a matter of choice? We ought to find out for ourselves what actual freedom is.

There is freedom *from* something, from pain, from anxiety. Is there freedom, not from something? If it is freedom from something, it is merely a reaction. It is like a man in prison saying, "I must get out of my prison." Psychologically, we live in a prison, and when it is painful, ugly, not satisfactory, then we want freedom from that. So we are saying that wanting freedom *from* something is the same thing as being in prison. What is that sense of deep, inward, authentic, unshakable freedom that is not *from* something? What is that freedom?

Let's together inquire into what freedom is. Everyone wants to escape from something. Most people are very lonely, and they want to escape from it through various forms of entertainment, religious and otherwise. But is there a freedom that is not a reaction? To find that out, one has to ask what love is. Is love a reaction? Is love attraction, whether it be sexual or otherwise? Please ask those questions of yourself to find the right answer.

How do you find the right answer to a question? When there is a question, you naturally reply to that question. If you are at all thinking, going along with the question, then you respond to that question. Then your response is answered. This is really dialogue. Then you respond to my response. So there is both question and answer, answer and question. If we maintain this answer, question, question, answer seriously, intensely, then in that process you disappear and the speaker disappears, and only the question remains. Then that very question has vitality. Test it out for yourself. It is like a rosebud; if the question is left in the air, as it were, then it is like a bud that gradually unfolds and shows its nature. The depth of a question has its own vitality, energy, drive. That is a dialogue, not just accepting what the other person is saying.

Is freedom that is not *from* something, love? And is love a reaction? For most of us, perhaps, love may not exist. Please, I am just asking this, I am not saying it does not exist. Perhaps most of us do not know what it means. We know attraction, we know tenderness, we know pity, we know guilt, remorse, and jealousy. Is all that love? If it is not love, then love has no reaction. Then that is freedom, which is not born out of a reaction. . . .This is very important to understand, not intellectually, not verbally, but to see the depth and the beauty of it.

When we are talking about the art of living, we should also ask what beauty is. When you see great architecture, the cathedrals of Europe, the great temples and the mosques of the world, constructed by great architects, great painters, the great sculptors like Michelangelo, that is beauty. So is beauty man-made? Please exercise your brain to find out . A tiger is not man-made. Thank the Lord! A tree in a field, alone, solitary, with all the dignity of a marvelous old tree, is not man-made. But the moment you paint that tree, that is man-made, and you admire it, go to a museum to see the tree painted by a great artist. So another part of the art of living is to understand the depth and the beauty of freedom, and the goodness of it. The aesthetic quality in life is born of sensitivity, is born out of all the senses in action, not one particular sense, but the whole move ment of the senses. Surely beauty is when! the self is not. When I am not, beauty is. When the self is not, love is.

And so love, freedom, goodness, beauty, are one, not separate. They are all interrelated. That word, *goodness*, is very old fashioned. There is extraordinary depth to that word. The depth of goodness can be felt only when there is freedom, when there is love, beauty.

What is desire? What is the source of desire? Where does desire spring from? Is desire born from the object perceived? I see a beautiful car. Does the seeing create the desire? Please be careful; don't agree with what I am saying. We are going to contradict all that presently, so don't be caught in a trap. Does the object create desire? I see a beautiful house, and I say, "My god, I wish I had that."

We ought to inquire very carefully into what desire is. We are not saying to suppress desire, or give in to desire. We ought together to find out for ourselves, not be told, what desire is. You see an object, a car, or a woman, or a beautiful tree in a lovely garden, and you say, "My god, I wish I had a garden like that." Don't you know that kind of desire? You see something; then from that seeing there is sensation. From that sensation what takes place? Contact is part of sensation. If you have heard this before, don't repeat it, because then that means nothing. Seeing, contact, sensation—now, what takes place after that? Go very slowly, find out. I see a very good watch in the window. I go inside, examine it, touch it, feel it, feel the weight of it, see who made it. And then what happens? Then thought comes in, creates an image and says, "I wish I had it." That is, seeing, contact, sensation, then thought immediately creates the image; and then when thought creates the image of me having that watch, at that second desire is born.

Now, if you see that, can there be an interval between seeing, contact, sensation? An interval before thought takes shape, makes a shape of it? Can you do it? It is all so rapid. When you slow it down, like a motion picture, then you see everything in detail. That is desire. So extend the gap. You are desire, you are the very structure of thought and desire. So if you understand, if you look into the nature of thought and your reactions, you can slow the whole mechanism down, so it is very quiet; or you understand this instantly. That requires attention, that requires passion to find out.

If we understand the nature and the structure of desire, then we can find out what meditation is. Is conscious meditation, meditation? Obviously not. If I consciously sit down for twenty minutes in the morning, twenty minutes in the afternoon, twenty minutes in the evening, then it becomes a relaxation, a nice, comfortable, enjoyable siesta. So what is meditation? If you consciously meditate, it has a direction, a motive, a desire to achieve. Surely that is not meditation, is it? That is like a clerk becoming a manager. The two things are the same: you call one "business," the other you call "religious achievement," but both are exactly the same thing.

Do those who meditate see that? Of course not. That means giving up their pet enjoyment, pet entertainment.

We are saying that conscious meditation is not meditation because it is born of desire to achieve, to become something, which is the self becoming something, the self, the "me" becoming god. It sounds so silly. Forgive me for using that word. Then: what is meditation? If it is not conscious meditation, then what is meditation? The word meditation means to ponder, to think over, and also to measure. That is part of the root meaning of *meditation* in Sanskrit. Now, can your brain stop measuring? I am this, I will be that. I am comparing myself with you—you are so beautiful, you have grace, you have brains, you have got quality, depth, you are wearing something extraordinary—and I am not that. That is measuring, which is comparison. Can you stop comparing? Don't agree. Stop comparing, and find out what it means to live without a movement of comparison.

So meditation is not a conscious, deliberate act. There is a totally different kind of meditation that has nothing whatsoever to do with thought and desire. And that means a brain that is really, if I may use the word, empty. Empty of all the things that thought, humankind, has made. And where there is space. Because freedom means that, love means that—space, vast, limitless space. And where there is space, there is silence and energy. If you are thinking about yourself all day long, which most of us are, then you have reduced the extraordinary capacity of the brain to such a small issue about yourself. Therefore you have no space.

The speaker is not a specialist on brains, but he has lived a long time studying by himself and watching others. The brain has its own rhythm that can be left alone. But when the brain is silent, not chattering, is utterly quiet, then there is that which is not measurable by words, that which is eternal, nameless.

So, you under stand, love is not a reaction, therefore it is free. Where there is love there is intelligence not born out of thought. Intelligence is something outside the brain. Compassion, love, freedom is outside the brain. Because the brain is conditioned, it cannot contain this.

[11]

THE BENEDICTION OF MEDITATION

WHAT IS living? Not what should living be, not what is the purpose of living, not what is the significance of living, not what is the principle upon which life should be based, not what is the goal of living, but actually what is living as it is now, as it is in our daily life? What is it actually in our private, secret daily life? Because that is the only fact, and all other things are unreal, illusory, theoretical. So what is this life, our life, the life of a private human being, the life of a human being in relationship with society, the society that people have made, which people have built. That society holds us prisoner. So we are the society, we are the world, and the world is not different from us. Which again is fairly obvious.

We are dealing not with abstractions, not with ideals, which are idiotic anyhow, but with what actually is, which is our living. What is our living? If you observe, from the moment we are born until we die it is a constant battle, constant struggle, with great pleasures, great fears, despair, loneliness, the utter lack of love, boredom, repetition, routine. Our life is the drudgery, the dullness, the boredom of spending forty years in an office or in a factory, being a housewife, the sexual pleasure, the jealousy, the envy, the failure of success and the worship of success. That is our daily tortured life, if you are at all serious and observe what actually is; but if you merely seek entertainment in different forms, whether it is in a church or on a football field, then such entertainment has its own pains, has its own problems. A superficial mind does escape through the church and through the football field because it is really not interested. Life is serious, and in that seriousness there is great laughter. And it is only the serious mind that is living, that can solve the immense problem of existence.

So our life as it is lived daily is a travail, and no one can deny it. And we don't know what to do about it. We want to find a way of living differently—at least, some of us say we must and make an attempt. Before making an attempt, before trying to change, we must understand what actually is, not what should be. We must actually take *what is* in our hands and look at it. And you cannot look at it, come into intimate contact with it, if you have an ideal, or if you are concerned with changing it. But if you are capable of looking at it as it is, then you will find there comes quite a different quality of change, and that is what we are going into now.

First see, actually—not shyly, or with reluctance, or with pain, or with resistance—what life is actually at this moment, every day. It is a travail. Can we look at it, can we live with it, be in intimate contact with it, be in direct relationship with it? Here comes the problem: to be directly in relation to something there must be no image between you and the thing you observe. The image is the word, the symbol, the memory of what it was yesterday, or a thousand yesterdays. That is, to put it very simply, the relationship that one has with one's wife or husband is a relationship based on an image—the image being accumulated through many years of pleasure, sex, nagging, dullness, repetition, domination, and so on. You have the image about her, and she has the image about you, and the contact between these two images is called "relationship." And obviously that is not relationship, but we have accepted it as relationship. So there is no direct contact with another human being.

In the same way, there is no direct contact with the actual, with *what is*. There is always the observer and the thing observed, and there is a division between them. It seems complex, but it is not if you listen quietly. And this division, or the screen in between, is the word, is the memory, is the space in which all conflict takes place. That space is the ego, is the "me." The "me" is the accumulated image, memory, thought of a thousand yesterdays, so there is no direct contact with *what is*. You either condemn *what is*, or rationalize *what is*, or accept it, or justify it, which are all verbalizations; and therefore there is no direct contact. And therefore there is no understanding and the resolution of *what is*.

I will explain this briefly and I hope it will be clear. One is conditioned to accept envy, envy being measurement, comparison. Someone is bright, intelligent, has success, been applauded, and the other, I, have not. Through comparison, through measurement, envy is cultivated from childhood. So there is envy as an object, as something outside of oneself, and one observes it, being envious. But envy is the observer; there is no division between the observer and the observed. The observer is the envy; and the observer cannot possibly do anything about envy because he is the cause and the effect, which is envy. So the *what is*, which is our daily life, with all its problems, fear, envy, jealousy, the utter despair, the loneliness, is not different from the observer who says, "I am lonely." The observer is lonely, the observer is envy, is fear. Therefore the observer cannot possibly do anything about *what is*. Which does not mean he accepts *what is*, which does not mean he is contented with *what is*. But when there is no conflict with *what is*, the conflict brought about through the division between the observer and the observed, when there is no resistance to *what is*, then you will find there is a complete transformation.

And that is meditation: to find out for yourself the whole structure and the nature of the observer, which is yourself. The observer is the observed, which is part of you. To realize the totality of this, the unity of this, is meditation in which there is no conflict whatsoever. And therefore, there is the dissolution, going beyond what is.

Then you will ask yourself: what is love? We are going to consider love together, though that word is heavily loaded, so trodden upon, so spoilt by the politician, by the priest, by every magazine that talks about it. What is love? Not what it should be, not what is the ideal, not the ultimate, but the love that we have, what is it? In the thing that we know, which we call "love," there is hate, jealousy, tremendous torture. We are not being cynical but merely observing actually *what is*, what the thing that we call love is. Is love hate? Is love jealousy? Is love possessiveness or the domination of the wife or the husband?

One says that one loves one's family, one's children. Do you love your children? If you loved your children with your heart, not with your shoddy little minds, do you think there would be a war tomorrow? If you loved your children, would you educate them to make them conform to a rotten society, train them, force them to accept the established order? If you really loved your children, would you allow them to be killed horribly in a war? As you observe all this, it indicates that there is no love at all. Love isn't sentiment, love isn't emotional nonsense. And above all, love isn't pleasure.

We must understand pleasure, because for us, love, sex and pleasure are involved. When we talk about love, we mean the enjoyment of sex, pleasure. And also it involves pain, torture. Please bear in mind that we are not denying pleasure. It is a pleasure to see lovely mountains lit by the setting sun, to see marvelous trees that have withstood fire, to see the dust of many months washed away by the rain, to see the stars. But to us that is not pleasure. What we are concerned with as pleasure is sensuous pleasure and the pleasure that we derive from something intellectual, emotional, and so on.

Pleasure, like fear, is engendered by thought. You have an experience of yesterday as you stood in a still valley, looking at all the marvel of the hills in that silence. There was great delight and pleasure at the moment. Then thought comes in and says, how nice it would be to repeat it. Thinking about that experience of yesterday, whether it be the looking at the lovely tree and the sky and the hills, or thinking about the sex that you enjoyed last night, is pleasure. Thought thinking about that which gave a delight yesterday, thinking about it, living in thought, in image, is the beginning of pleasure. And you think about what might happen, about pleasure being denied tomorrow. You might lose your job, there might be an accident, ill health; thinking about it is pain, is fear.

So thought creates both fear and pleasure. To us love is thought, because love to us is pleasure, and pleasure is the outcome of thought, is nourished by thought. It is not the actual moment of seeing the sunset, or the sexual act, but thinking about it that is pleasure. So to us love is engendered by thought, nourished by thought, sustained and prolonged as pleasure by thought. When you look very closely, it is an obvious fact, not to be denied.

So, one asks: is love thought? Can thought cultivate love, or can it cultivate pleasure? It can cultivate pleasure, but it cannot possibly under any circumstances cultivate love, any more than thought can cultivate humility. So love is not pleasure. Love is not desire. But you cannot deny desire or pleasure. When you look at the world, at the beauty of a tree or the beauty of a face, there is great pleasure, enjoyment at the moment, but thought interferes and gives it a space and time to flourish as memory and pleasure. When you realize this, understand the structure and the nature of pleasure in relation to love—an understanding that is part of meditation—then you will find that love is something entirely different. Then you will really love your children, then you will really create a new world. When yoJ know love, do what you will, there is no wrong. It is only when you are pursuing pleasure, as you are, that everything goes wrong.

Another problem is death. We have considered what actual, everyday living is. We have taken a journey deeply within ourselves to find out what love is, and we are also going to find out what death means. You will understand this really great problem if you know how to die. If you know how to die, then what lies beyond death, what happens after death, is irrelevant. So we are going to find out.

Death is inevitable. Any machinery, any organism that is being constantly used, will inevitably come to an end through old age, disease. Old age to us is a horror. I do not know if you have ever noticed how in the autumn a leaf falls from the tree, how beautiful it is, what lovely color, what gentleness it has, full of beauty, so easily destroyed. And with us, as we grow old, we look at ourselves, the pretensions, the disfigurement, the ugliness. Old age becomes a problem, because we have not lived rightly in our youth, in our middle age. We have never lived at all because we are frightened. We are frightened of living and frightened of dying. And as we grow old everything happens to us.

We are going to find out what it means to die, knowing that the organism comes to an end, and knowing that the mind, in its despair of coming to an end, will inevitably seek a hope, a comfort in some theory of resurrection or reincarnation. You know the whole of Asia is conditioned to accept that theory, reincarnation. They talk about it a great deal, write about it. They have invested their whole life in the hope of a new life in a next life. But they forget one final ultimate thing; that is, if you are going to be born in a next life, you must live this life rightly. Therefore it means it matters tremendously what you do in this life, how you live, what you do, what you think, how you talk, how your thoughts function. If you do not live rightly now, in a next life you would have the reward of not living rightly, which is punishment. But they forget all that, and talk about the beauty of reincarnation, justice, and all that trivial nonsense.

So we are not escaping from the fact through some theory, but facing the fact without fear. Knowing the organism comes to an end, what does it mean to die psychologically, inwardly? In dying, there is no argument; you cannot say, "Wait a few days more, please, I haven't finished my book; I haven't become the chief executive of some organization; I haven't become the archbishop, hold on a minute." You cannot argue. So one has to find out inwardly, psychologically, how to die; that is to end all the past, all the pleasures, the remembrance that you have cherished, the things that you hold on to. To die every day. Not in theory, but actually. To die to the pleasure that you had yesterday, which means die immediately to that pleasure, not give it a continuance. To live that way, so that the mind is always fresh, young and innocent, vulnerable, is meditation.

If you have laid the foundation of virtue, which is order in relationship, and when there is this quality of love and dying, which is all of life, then the mind becomes extraordinarily quiet, silent, naturally, not enforced through discipline, through control, through suppression. Then that silence is immensely rich. Beyond that, no word, no description is of any avail. Then the mind does not inquire into the absolute because it has no need to inquire. For in that silence there is that which is.

And the whole of this is the benediction of meditation.

[12]

LIFE BECOMES AN EXTRAORDINARY THING

THERE IS the art of listening, there is the art of learning, there is the art of perception. The art of listening is not merely hearing words. Hearing the words is quite a different process from the art of listening. The art of listening implies that you are actually listening, not interpreting, not agreeing, not putting up resistance, but listening to what another has to say, so that you are not the translator of what is being said. You don't project your own conclusions, prejudices, opinions, judgments; you are actually listening. That requires a certain attention, and in that attention you as the listener disappear, there is just listening. When we listen attentively there is neither agreement nor nonagreement; we are just in a state of attention. Listen not only to what the speaker is saying but also listen to your wife or husband, which is much more difficult because you have become used to each other. But fortunately you don't know the speaker, the speaker doesn't know you, so we can both listen without any prejudices. It implies great sensitivity to have your senses active so that you are listening completely. If one listens so attentively, there is a certain miracle taking place. It is not a listening to one opinion against another opinion, or argument against another argument, however reasonable, however crooked, illusory, but a listening in which there is silence.

Listen so that you listen with your senses naturally, not just with the hearing of the ear but with all your senses awakened. Then you do not exist, only the sound. Sound has an extraordinary importance in life. There is the sound of the sea, the sound of the voice of your wife or husband, the sound among the leaves, the sound of the waves, the sound of a tree that is very still. Sound has extraordinary importance.

And there is the art of learning. The art of learning is not the accumulation of memory. You go to school where you cultivate memory, learn mathematics, biology, physics, and so on. You are being informed. Your brain is gathering information, storing knowledge about mathematics or geography, history, whatever you like, and that knowledge remains stored in the brain to be used skillfully or not skillfully in earning a livelihood. So knowledge is static. You can add to it, you can take away from it, but the core of it is static, it is not dynamic. That which is dynamic cannot be added to or taken away from, inherently it is dynamic; but knowledge is not. Knowledge is mere accumulation of information, storing the result of many experiences. That which is kept is not dynamic; that which is moving like a river is dynamic.

If you want to be an engineer, flier, or a physicist, you must accumulate knowledge; that is necessary, but it is adding to what is already known, so knowledge gradually becomes static. Whereas, in the act of learning you are moving, never remaining in the same place. Learning is the application now of what is being said and discovering for yourself whether it is true or false. If it is true, act.

In the world, theory and action (or life) have nothing to do with each other. You are full of theories, full of probabilities, possibilities; you say one thing, do another. You know the game you play. So learning is something that is whole, not fragmented as knowledge is. Learning is a movement like a river with tremendous volume moving.

Then there is the art of perception. Perception is different from seeing. Perception is not of time, but the seeing and the translating what has been seen into action involves a certain period of time. I see what I should do, and I will do it. Between the seeing and the doing, there is a gap, an interval, which is time. You see something that should be done and you think about it, you argue, probe, see whether it is convenient or not convenient, profitable or not, and so on. All that implies an interval of time before action. Whereas perception is seeing and doing so that there is no interval between action and perception. I see, I perceive that I should not be a Hindu because one of the reasons for being a Hindu is for security, and also it is one of the causes of war. Nationalism, tribalism, is one of the causes of war. So I see that, I perceive it to be the truth and therefore I am no longer a Hindu. If you see the danger of being a Muslim, Hindu, Buddhist, Christian, and so on, you act instantly, as you act instantly when you see a cobra.

So there is the art of listening, the art of learning, and the art of perception. If one lives with this art, then life becomes an extraordinary thing. That requires great sensitivity, care, attention.

[13]

THE ART OF DYING

AS YOU ARE, most human beings throughout the world are afraid of death. That is one of the fundamental fears of life. We all know that death is for everybody, for you and me. That is an absolute certainty. You cannot escape from that. You might live longer by not wasting your energy, by leading a simple, sane, rational life; but whatever the way you live, death is inevitable. It is a fact.

Would you face that fact? You are going to die, so is the speaker. "You," who are you? Who are you, sirs, and ladies, who are you? You have money, you have position, you have capacity, you have dishonesty, your confusions, your anxiety, your loneliness, your bank account. You are all that, aren't you? Be simple and honest. It is so. And we are asking, what is the art of living when we are going to die? What is the art of living so that one is not afraid of death?

Let's go into it, not intellectually, not theoretically, but actually, so that you know what death means. We are not advocating suicide. There are certain philosophers, the existentialists and others, who say life is a perpetual going up the hill and coming down the hill, pushing up the hill, and after you reach a certain height coming down. They say that such a life has no meaning, therefore commit suicide. We are not saying that is the way to live. That is not the art of living. We are asking ourselves why we are afraid of death. Whether we are young, old, and so on, why is there this torment of which we are so afraid? It may be conscious or unconscious. And the fear of death is also suffering, suffering in leaving my family, suffering in leaving all the things I have accumulated.

So the art of living is not only to find out how to live our daily life, but also to find out what the significance of death is, while living. What is death? There is the biological, organic ending through disease, through old age, accident, through some misfortune. What do we mean by dying? If we can understand that, then life and death can live together; then death is not at the end when the organism ends, but you live with death and life together.

Ask that question. Put to yourself this question of whether it is possible to live, live the art of living, living with death. To find that out, you must find out what living is. Which is more important, living or dying, before or after? Most people are concerned with after, whether there is reincarnation, all that kind of stuff. But they never ask about the living, which, is more important, which is an art. If there is right living, perhaps death is also parti of right living, not at the end of one's stupid life.

So, what is living. We can discuss it, have a dialogue about it, but you have to answer that question for yourself. What is your life? What is your daily life, which is what your life is; it is a long series of daily lives. What are those lives? Pain, anxiety, insecurity, uncertainty, some kind of illusory devotion to some entity that we have invented, some kind of fanciful, illusory existence, a make-believe life, having faith, having belief. All that is what you are. Youl are attached to your house, to your money, to your bank, to your wife, children. You are attached; this is your life. You live a constant struggle, with constant effort, discomfort, pain, loneliness, sorrow. That is your life. And you are afraid to let that go. And death says, "My friend, you cannot take it with you." You cannot take your money, your family, your knowledge, your beliefs. Death says you have to leave all that behind. Would you agree, or do you deny that? Face it.

Death says to me, "When I come you have to let go." Now, is it possible for me, living, to let go? Will you let go? I am attached to my furniture. I have polished it, I have looked after it, I won't give it away; it is mine, it is part of me. When I am attached to a piece of furniture, that furniture is me. Death says, "My friend, you can't take that desk with you." So can you be totally free, totally free of attachment to that piece of furniture? That is death. So you are living and dying, all the time.

See the beauty of it. See the freedom that gives you, the energy, the capacity. When you are attached there is fear, there is anxiety, uncertainty, and uncertainly, fear, causes sorrow.

Sorrow is part of life. Everyone on earth has suffered, has shed tears. Haven't you shed tears? Your husband doesn't care for you, he uses you and you use him. And you suddenly realize how ugly that is, and you suffer. People have killed each other throughout history in the name of religion, in the name of god, in the name of nationality. So humanity has suffered immensely. And they have never been able to solve that problem, never solved *suffering*. Where there is suffering there is no love. In suffering there is not only self-pity, there is also fear of loneliness, of separation, of divisions. Remorse, guilt, all that is contained in that word, suffering. And we have never solved this problem. We put up with it, we shed tears and carry the memory of the son, the brother, the wife, or the husband for the rest of our life. Is there an end to sorrow? Or must we forever and ever carry this burden? To find that out is also the art of living. The art of living is to have no fear. And also the art of living is to have no sorrow.

One of the problems of life is to see whether it is possible to live without sorrow. What is sorrow? When my son dies, something has broken in me, especially if I am a woman. I have borne him in my womb, given birth, and I have nursed him, looked after him—and the pain of all that, the pleasure of it, the joy of the mother— and then he ends up being killed. For your country, he will be killed. Why do you allow it?

So what is sorrow? Is it that my son has gone, can never return? Though I think we will meet in a next life, he is gone. That is a fact. But I carry the memory, I keep his picture near my heart. I live on that memory, shedding tears, I cannot forget. It is part of my burden. We have never inquired into sorrow, into suffering, and asked whether it can ever end, not at the end of one's life, but now, today.

Is the cause of sorrow self-pity? Is it that my son was young, fresh, alive, and now is gone? Is it that I am attached to him? Face all this. What is that attachment? To whom am I attached? To my son? What do I mean by "my son"? Be rational, logical. What is my son? I have a picture of him, I have an image of him, I want him to be something. He is my son, and I am attached desperately because he will carry on my business, he will be better at getting more money. I also have a certain affection, we will not call it love, but we will call it a certain kind of affection. If you loved your son you would have a different kind of education, a different kind of upbringing, not just to follow in your footsteps. He is the new generation, and a new generation may be totally different from yours. I hope he is. I want him to be a new generation, of a different type of person than me. I want him to inherit my money, my possessions, my house. And when he dies, everything goes. How cruel all this is. And this is one of the causes of great sorrow.

And death, of course, is the final sorrow. But if you are living with death and life together, then there is no change. You are incarnating every day afresh—not "you," a new thing is incarnating every day afresh. And in that there is great beauty. That is creation. In that there is tremendous freedom. And the root meaning of the word freedom is love. The art of living and the art of dying, together, bring about great love. And love has its own intelligence, not the intelligence of a cunning mind. Intelligence is something outside of the brain.

[14]

SEEING IS THE ONLY TRUTH

IT IS very important to observe. It is quite an art, to which one must give a great deal of attention. We see only very partially, we never see anything completely, with the totality of our mind, or with the fullness of our heart. Unless we learn this extraordinary art, it seems to me that we shall be functioning, living, through a very small part of our mind, through a small segment of the brain.

For various reasons, we never see anything completely. Because we are so concerned with our own problems, or we are so conditioned, so heavily burdened with belief, with tradition, with the past, it actually prevents us from seeing or listening. We never see a tree except through the image that we have of it, the concept of that tree; but the concept, the knowledge, the experience, is entirely different from the actual tree. Look at a tree and you will find how extraordinarily difficult it is to see it completely, so that no image, no screen, comes between the seeing and the actual fact. By completely I mean with the totality of your mind and heart, not a fragment of it. We are either emotional, sentimental, or very intellectual, which obviously prevents us from actually seeing the color, the beauty of the light, the trees, the birds. We never are in direct relationship with any of this.

I doubt very much if we are in relationship with anything, even with our own ideas, thoughts, motives, impressions; there is always the image that is observing, even when we observe ourselves.

It is very important to understand that the act of seeing is the only truth; there is nothing else. If I know how to see a tree, j or a bird, or a lovely face, or the smile of a child, there it is, I don't have to do anything more. But that seeing of the bird, of the leaf, listening to the noise of birds, becomes almost impossible because of the image that one has built, not only about nature but also about others. These images actually prevent us from seeing and feeling, feeling being entirely different from sentimentality and emotion.

As we said, we see everything fragmentarily. We are trained from childhood to look, to observe, to learn, to live, in a fragment. And there is the vast expanse of the mind that we never touch or know. That mind is vast, immeasurable, but we never touch it; we do not know the quality of it because we have never looked at anything completely, with the totality of our mind, of our heart, of our nerves, of our eyes, of our ears. To us the word, the concept, is extraordinarily important, not the acts of seeing and doing. But conceptual living, that is, having the concept, which is a belief, an idea, prevents us from actually seeing, doing; and therefore we say we have problems of action, of what to do or not to do. Conflict arises between the act and the concept.

Do please observe what I am talking about, not merely hear the words, but observe yourselves, using the speaker as a mirror in which you can see yourself. What the speaker has to say is of very little importance, and the speaker himself is of no importance whatsoever, but what you gather out of observing yourself is important, because there must be a total revolution, a complete mutation in our minds, in our way of living, in our feeling, in the activities of our daily life. And to bring about such fundamental, deep revolution is possible only when you know how to look; because when you do look, you are looking not only with your eyes and nerves, but you are also seeing with your heart, with your mind. And you cannot see completely in this way if you are living, functioning, thinking, acting within a fragment of the total mind.

Look at what is happening in the world. We are being conditioned by society, by the culture in which we live, and that culture is the product of humanity. There is nothing holy, or divine, or eternal about culture. Culture, society, books, radios, all that we listen to and see, the many influences of which we are either conscious or unconscious, all these encourage us to live within a very small fragment of the vast field of the mind. You go through school, college, and learn a technique to earn a living; for the next forty or fifty years you spend your life, your time, your energy, your thought, in that specialized little field. There is the vast field of the mind, and unless we bring about a radical change in this fragmentation, there can be no revolution at all. There will be economic, social, and so-called cultural modifications, but human beings will go on suffering, will go on in conflict, in war, in misery, in sorrow, and in despair.

You can be a clever lawyer, a first-class engineer, or an artist, or a great scientist, but it is always within a fragment of the whole. Actually see what is taking place. The communists are doing it, the capitalists are doing it, parents, schools, education are all shaping the mind to function within a certain pattern, a certain fragment. And we are always concerned with bringing about a change only within the pattern, within the fragment.

How is one to realize this, not theoretically, not as a mere idea, but see the actuality of it, see the actual? The actual is what is taking place every day and is spoken of in newspapers, by politicians, through culture and tradition, in the family. When you see, you must question yourself. I am sure you would if you saw, and that is why it is very important to understand how you see. If you really saw the fragmentation, then the question would be, "How can the totalj mind act?" I do not mean the fragment, not the conditioned mind, nor the educated, sophisticated mind, the mind that is afraid, the mind that says, "There is God," or "There is no God"; "There is my family, your family, my nation, your nation."

Then you will ask how this totality of the mind can be, how it can function completely, even while learning a technique. It has to learn a technique and to live in relationship with others in our present disordered society. Bearing that in mind, one must ask the fundamental question, "How can this totality of the mind be made completely sensitive, so that even the fragment becomes sensitive?"

At present, we are not sensitive; there are spots in this field that are sensitive, but when our particular personality, our particular idiosyncrasy, or our particular pleasures are denied, then there is a battle. We are sensitive in fragments, in spots, but we are not sensitive completely. So the question is, how can the fragment, which is part of the total, which is being made dull every day by repetition, also be made sensitive as well as the total?

You may never have asked yourself about it, because we are all satisfied to live with as little trouble and conflict as possible in that little part of that field that is our life, appraising the marvelous culture of that little part as opposed to other cultures. We are not even aware what the implications are of living in a tiny fragment, a corner of a very vast field. We don't see for ourselves how deeply we are concerned with the little part, and we are trying to find answers to the problem within that fragment, within that little corner of this vast life. We ask ourselves how the mind, which is now half asleep in this vast field, because we are concerned only with the little part, can become totally aware of this whole thing, become completely sensitive.

There is no method, because any method, system, repetition, or habit, is essentially part of the corner of that field. The first thing is to see the actual fact of the little corner and what its demands are. Then we can ask how we can make the whole field completely sensitive, because in that lies the only true revolution. When there is total sensitivity of the whole of the mind, then we will act differently; our thinking, feeling, will be wholly of a different dimension. But there is no method. Don't ask, "How am I to arrive, achieve, become sensitive?" You cannot go to college to become sensitive; you cannot read books or be told what to do to become sensitive. This is what you have been doing within that corner of the field, and it has made you more and more insensitive. This can be seen in your daily life, with its callousness, brutality, and violence. We become callous because we are functioning, living, acting, within the small, petty little corner of a distorted field.

There is no method. Please do realize this, because when you realize it, you are free of the enormous weight of all authority, and so free of the past. The past is implicit in our culture, which we think is so wonderful—the traditions, the beliefs, the memories. All that is put aside completely, forever, when you realize there is no method of any kind to bring freedom from the "little corner." But you have to learn all about the little corner. Then you are free of the burden that makes you insensitive.

Now, as there is no method, what is one to do? Method implies practice, dependence, your method, my method, one person's path and another's path. The problem is that we do not know the depth and the immensity of the mind. You can read about it. You can read the modern psychologists, or the ancient teachers who have talked about it. Distrust them, because it is you yourself who have to find out, not according to somebody else. We do not know the mind, we cannot have any concept about it. You cannot have any ideas, any opinions, any knowledge about it. So you are free from any supposition, from any theology.

So, once again, what is one to do? All that one has to do is to see. See the corner, the little house that one has built in a corner of a vast, immeasurable field, and is living there, fighting, quarrelling, "improving." You know all that is going on there. See it!

That is why it is very important to understand what it means to see, because the moment there is conflict you belong to that isolated corner. Where there is seeing there is no conflict. That is why one has to learn from the very beginning—no, not from the beginning, but now—to see. Not tomorrow, because there is no tomorrow. It is only the search for pleasure, or fear, or pain that invents "tomorrow." Actually there is no tomorrow psychologically, but the brain, the mind, has invented time.

What one has to do is to see. You cannot see if you are not sensitive, and you are not sensitive if you have an image between you and the thing seen. Seeing is the act of love. You know what makes the total mind sensitive? Only love. You can learn a technique and yet love; but if you have technique and no love you are going to destroy the world. Do watch it in yourselves, do go into it in your own minds and hearts and you will see it for yourselves. Seeing, observing, listening are the greatest acts. If you are looking out from that little corner, you cannot see what is happening in the world—the despair, the anxiety, the aching loneliness, the tears of the mothers, wives, lovers, of those people who have been killed. You have to see all this, neither emotionally nor sentimentally, not saying, "I am against war," or "I am for war," because sentimentality and emotionalism are the most destructive things. Thfl avoid facts and so avoid *what is*.

So, the seeing is all important. The seeing is the understanding. You cannot understand through the mind, through the intellect, or understand through a fragment. There is understanding only whenj the mind is completely quiet, which means when there is no image.

Seeing destroys all barriers. As long as there is separation between you and the tree, between you and me, and between you and your neighbor—the neighbor a thousand miles away or next door—there must be conflict. Separation means conflict, that is very simple. And we have lived in conflict; we are used to conflict and to separation. India sees itself as a geographical, political, economical, social, cultural unit, and the same goes for Europe, and America, and Russia. They see separate units, each against the other, and all this separation is bound to breed war. This does not mean that we must all agree, or if we disagree that I am doing battle with you. There is no disagreement whatsoever, or agreement, when you see something as it is. It is only when you have opinions about what you see that there is disagreement and that there is separation.

In seeing a tree, when you actually see it, there is no division between you and the tree, there is no observer seeing the tree. Observe for yourself a tree, a flower, the face of a person. Look at any one of them, and so look that the space between you and them is nonexistent. And you can only look that way when there is love, that word that has been so misused. When you have this sense of real observation, real seeing, then that seeing brings with it extraordinary elimination of time and space, which comes about when there is love. And you cannot have love without recognizing beauty. You may talk about beauty, write, design, but if you have no love, nothing is beautiful. Being without love means that you are not totally sensitive. And because you are not totally sensitive you are degenerating. You are degenerate ing because you are not sensitive to the whole process of living.

Our fundamental problem then is not how to stop wars, not which "God" is better, not which political system or economic system is better, not which party is worth voting for. The most fundamental problem for the human being, whether he is in America, India, Russia, or anywhere else, is this question of freedom from "the little corner." And that little corner is ourselves, that little corner is your shoddy little mind. We have made that little corner, because our own little minds are fragmented and therefore incapable of being sensitive to the whole. We want that little part to be made safe, peaceful, quiet, satisfying, pleasurable—thereby avoiding all pain, because, fundamentally, we are seeking pleasure. If you have examined pleasure, your own pleasure, have observed it, watched it, gone into it, you see that where there is pleasure, there is pain. You cannot have one without the other; and we are always demanding more pleasure and therefore inviting more pain. And on that we have built this part, which we call human life. Seeing is to be intimately in contact with it, and you cannot be intimately, actually in contact with it if you have concepts, beliefs, dogmas, or opinions.

So what is important is to see and to listen. Listen to the birds, listen to your wife's voice, however irritating, beautiful or ugly. Listen to it and listen to your own voice, however beautiful, ugly, or impatient it may be. Then out of this listening you will find that all separation between the observer and the observed comes to an end. Therefore no conflict exists and you observe so carefully that the very observation is discipline; you do not have to impose discipline. And that is the beauty, if you only realize it; that is the beauty of seeing. If you can see, you have nothing else to do, because in that seeing there is all discipline, all virtue, which is attention.

And in that seeing there is all beauty, and with beauty there is love. Then when there is love you have nothing more to do. Then where you are, you have heaven; then all seeking comes to an end.

[15]

LIFE WITHOUT A SHADOW OF CONTROL

WHAT PLACE has meditation in daily life? Or is meditation something separate from daily life? Is it an idea that you must meditate, that you must do this, that you must do that? Do you come to a conclusion and introduce that concept into daily life? Or do you try to find out what relationship action has with the total awareness of consciousness?

Why should one meditate at all? We lead our daily life rather unhappily, shoddily, in conflict, misery, suffering, deceived by others, and so on. That is our daily life. Why do we want to introduce meditation into that? Or is understanding the meaning, the structure, the reactions, of conflict, sorrow, arrogance, pride, and so on, part of meditation?

It is not that you meditate and then introduce it into action, into daily life, but rather that during daily life, when you go to the office, when you are working in the factory, or plowing a field, or talking to your wife, husband, girl, or boy, you are aware of your reactions. In the investigation and comprehension of those reactions—of why you are jealous, why a state of anxiety exists in you, why you accept authority, why you depend on another—that exploration itself is meditation. It is not the other way round, and it is not an intellectual understanding. If you meditate and then introduce what you think is meditation into daily life, there is conflict. You think this is so, and you are bringing that into action, into daily life, so there must be contradiction. Whereas if one is envious, as most of us are, seeing what the nature of envy is, why we are envious—not saying it is right or wrong, or that we should not be, or should be, but inquiring into why this envy arises and being free of it—is the movement of meditation. In that there is no conflict; you are inquiring constantly. This demands your attention; this demands that you must be serious, not just play with words.

So meditation has a place in daily life when there is an inquiry into the whole nature and structure of your being—your reactions, the state of your consciousness, why you believe, don't believe, why you are influenced by institutions, and so on.

All that is an actual movement of meditation. If one is actually, not theoretically, doing it, then you begin to understand the nature of consciousness. You are not imposing something on it according to Freud, according to some psychologist, some guru. You are inquiring into your whole being; that being is your consciousness.

I wonder if you have ever inquired into the whole movement of thought, the whole activity of thinking, and whether thought, thinking, can see itself moving. Please, this is rather important if you want to go into it, if you are at all serious in this matter. It is really very important to comprehend the question first. I can say, "I am aware of my consciousness," through my belief, through my fears, through my pleasures, through my sorrow. I can be aware of the content of my consciousness by saying, "Yes, I am afraid, I am greedy, I suffer, I am arrogant, I have pride," and so on, which is the content of consciousness of which I am aware. In doing that, "I" am different from my consciousness.

So there is the "me," the observer observing his consciousness. But the "me" is greedy, the "me" is anxious, the "me" is frightened, the "me" is full of anxiety, uncertainty, sorrow, which is my consciousness, so I am not different from my consciousness. I am not different from what I think. I am not different from the experiences I have had. I am not different or something totally opposite to my anxieties, fears, and all the rest of it. I am all that. I may think I am God, but the very thinking is part of me, which invents God.

So then, if the observer is the observed, which is the consciousness, the question arises, can that consciousness be aware of its own movements? To put it very simply, is there an awareness of the arising of anger, anger itself, so that there is not "me" different from anger? Let's go into it. One is angry; at the moment of anger there is no recognition of being angry. Have you noticed? At the second, at the moment of intense anger there is only that state. A second later you call it "anger." Which means that you have recognized from the past what has happened in the past, and what is happening now, and you say, "That is anger." At the moment of anger, there is no recognition and the naming of that reaction. A second later the naming begins. The naming is from the past; the naming is the recognition from the past of the present reaction. So can you not name the present reaction, but just observe without naming it? The moment you name it, you have recognized it and so strengthened the reaction. It is very interesting.

That is, the word is not the thing. The word tent is not the actual fact, but we are carried away by the word and not by the fact. So to comprehend, to see the fact that the word is not the thing is tremendously important. When there is anger, which is a reaction, to observe it without naming it so that reaction begins to wither away. The moment you name it you have strengthened it; the strengthening is from the past.

If that is clear, we can go the next step, which is, is it possible for the senses to be aware of themselves; not you sire aware of the senses, but the senses themselves open? Kindly observe in yourself the reactions of the senses. Now our senses function separately, seeing, tasting, hearing, smelling, and so on. They are all separate. Is there a total movement of all the senses together? This is really quite fascinating to find out, because then you will see if there is an observation of a person, of the movement of the waters of the sea, of the mountains, the birds, or your friend, or your intimate person, with all the senses. Then there is no center from which you are observing.

Please do it, test it out. Do not accept anything. Test it out for yourself. When you smell something lovely, the perfume of an early morning when the air is clean, washed by the rain, and there is beauty in the land, is one particular sense awake, or are you observing the total delicacy and the beauty of the morning with all your senses?

Understand the sensory responses, whether the sensory responses are broken up, or the senses all respond together. If there is response of a particular sense, sensation, then what takes place? When there is only the reaction of a scent through the nose, then all the other senses are more or less in abeyance. Test it, test it out. I am asking if, when you smell a flower, there is total response of all the senses, not only smell but the whole organism responding with its senses?

When you hear noise, do you respond completely, so that there is no resistance to the noise, there is no irritation from the noise, so you are totally with the noise? Do you look at mountains, which you may have looked at every evening and every morning, not only with your eyes, optically, but is there a perception of the mountains with all your senses? If there is, there is no center from which you are looking. Test it out. Look as though you are looking with all your being, with all your senses. Then you will see that you are looking at something for the first time, not with jaded eyes and memory and so on.

So the question arises, can thought be aware of itself? You are thinking now, aren't you? When I ask you a question, the whole movement of thinking arises. Right? Obviously. Now I am asking whether that thinking itself sees itself thinking? No, it is not possible.

You see, I am asking whether one can live a life without having a single conflict, a single effort, without any form of control. We live with effort, we struggle; there is always achieving, moving, and so our life is lived in constant struggle, constant battle, constant contradiction—"I must do this, I must not do that, I must control myself, why should I control myself, that is old-fashioned, I will do what I want to do." All that is a movement of violence. We are asking if it is possible to live without any shadow of control. Which does not mean doing everything you want to do. That is too childish, because you cannot. Where there is control there is conflict, there is a battle going on, which expresses itself in many, many different ways—violence, suppression, neuroticism, and permissiveness.

So I am asking myself and you whether we can live a daily life without a shadow of control. To live that way, I have to find out who the controller is. Is the controller different from the controlled? If they are both the same, there is no need for control.

If I am jealous because you have everything and I have nothing, from that jealousy arises anger, hatred, envy, a sense of violence. I want to have all that you have, and if I can't get it get bitter, angry, and all the rest follows. So can I live without jealousy, which means without comparison? Test it out. Can you live your daily life withow comparing at all? Of course there is comparing when I choose something to wear. I am not talking about that. I am talking about not having any sense of measurement psychologically, which is comparison. If you have no measurement at all, will you decay, will you become a vegetable, dd nothing, stagnate?

Because you are comparing, because you are struggling, you think you are living, but if you don't struggle it may be a totally different form of living.

[16]

IS THERE SOMETHING SACRED?

THE ART of living is to have complete freedom, not the freedom of choice, not the freedom of what one wants to do, or likes to do, for that freedom is limited by the environment, by society, by religious doctrines, and so on. Freedom is something entirely different. It is not freedom about something or from something, but freedom per se. When there is that freedom, there is the supreme way of living without any conflict, without any problem. There is heightened intelligence when the brain is fully active, not active in a particular direction, either scientific or business, or with the problems of daily life. When there is that freedom, there is great energy, tremendous energy.

The word *freedom* also, etymologically, means love. Freedom implies inquiry into the problem of relationship. In that relationship, whether it is most intimate or with the neighbor of a thousand miles away, as long as there is an image about the person with whom you are related or he has an image about you, there must be conflict, . . . The whole idea of freedom as choice, movement, status, position, achievement, success, is only a very small part of freedom. It may perhaps be a most destructive freedom if everyone does what he likes, as is happening throughout the world. It will bring about great chaos, which is what is going on.

We have lived with conflict for generation upon generation, not only in our relationships, but with society, with other nations. Nationalism is tribal worship and that is causing enormous despair, wars, divisions: the Jew and the Arab, the Hindu and the Muslim, the communist, the socialist, and the so-called democrat. There is tremendous conflict going on in the world. This is the society that human beings have built.

Society is not something that comes out of the air. The society in which we live is created by every human being, and in that society, which is immoral, there is a great deal of injustice. One questions whether there is any justice at all. Society is what we have made of it, and we are caught by that thing we have made. Unless there is a radical mutation, change, a fundamental psychological revolution—not physical revolutions, which have led humanity nowhere—society will remain as it is now. Change implies time, change from this to that, change from violence to nonviolence. To change violence into nonviolence takes a long duration of time. Will time change human beings? That is a very basic, radicfl question. In time, which is an evolution of fifty thousand years or more, has humanity changed psychologically during that long period? Obviously we have not. We are very primitive people, quarreling with each other, with endless wars, always in conflict. Psychologically, inwardly, we have changed very, very little. Perhaps, technologically we have advanced immensely, with the atom bomb, telecommunications, the extraordinary development of machinery, computers, and so on, but inwardly, deeply, we remain what we have been for ten thousand or more years. Time does not change human beings.

Why are people frightened of death? As you get older, either you become a very religious, superstitious human being, or join some cult, or you begin to inquire into what death is, and why we have separated it from living, why we postpone it, put it far away. Why do we human beings do all this? Is it fear of losing the known, entering into the unknown?

Is it possible to live with death? Please, don't answer. You have to understand what living is. Living, as far as we know, is one constant travail, with occasional pleasure, occasional comfort, and if you have money you are more or less secure, but there is always insecurity threatening. Going to the office every day from nine to five, struggling, competing, quarreling, hating, loving (which is called pleasure)—all that is our way of living. That is what we know, and we are frightened to let that go. Death means the ending of all that, not only the organism coming to an end, but also all the attachments, all the knowledge, experience. So can one live with death and life together, not separate? Which means, can you live with death so that there is no attachment? Death is going to wipe away all your attachments: your family, your knowledge, your becoming, your fame, all that nonsense. Can we, as we live our daily life, live with death, which is to be free of attachment, of competition, of psychological becoming, so that there is no interval between living and dying? Then, you have tremendous freedom and energy. Not to do more mischief, not to get more money, to become famous, that is rather childish—forgive me. When you live with something that has immense meaning, that is freedom.

From the most ancient of times, humanity has sought something beyond the daily existence with its monotony, with its routine, its mechanical habits both physical and inward. Man has said that there must be something beyond all this. So he invented God. God is invented by thought. If there is no fear of any kind psychologically, absolutely no fear, not a shadow of it, not a breath of it, then is God necessary?

Man has sought this; and the priests came along and said, "We will interpret it for you; we will organize it for you, you are ignorant, but we are learned." And the process of that is to dress up in costumes, to impress, and also create a great deal of show. The ancient Egyptians, and further back the Sumerians, seven or eight thousand years ago, had hell and heaven too. They said you must believe, otherwise you will go to hell, and they persecuted, killed, tortured. Christianity has done this: you must believe in Jesus, or you are a heretic. Doubt is not allowed in the Christian world. If you doubt, then the thing collapses. But in the Asiatic world, especially in India, one of the teachings is that you must question, you must doubt not only your guru but question yourself, have a dialogue, never accept. There is no authority except the authority of the truth, not the truth invented by books or by thought or by priests.

What is religion? If you wipe away all the nonsense and superstitions and beliefs of organized modern religions, and not be a Hindu, a Buddhist, or a Christian, it does not mean that you become an atheist. It means you are inquiring, questioning, asking, discussing, pushing, driving, flowing.

Then, is there something sacred? Is there something eternal that is beyond time? Is there something totally untouched by thought? Thought, the "you," cannot find out. Meditation is not just repeating some words; that is all too immature. Meditation is something extraordinary. Meditation is the understanding of the whole of life, both external and inward, the understanding of your daily life, your relationships, freeing yourself from fear, and questioning what the self, the "me," is. Is the "me" merely a bundle of memories and therefore has it no actuality? Please inquire into all this. That is all part of meditation.

The very word meditation, both in Sanskrit and in the ordinary dictionary, means to free the mind from all measurement, that is from becoming. "I am this, I will be that" is a measure. Measure is necessary for the whole technological world. Without measure we could not create a dynamo or the atom bomb, or build a car—but can we psychologically, inwardly, be free of all comparison, which is measurement? Can there be freedom from fear—from all the hurts that one has had from childhood, the psychological wounds that one keeps preciously, which distort our lives—freedom from sorrow, pain loneliness, depression, anxiety? Can one be free of the self, the "me," not at the end of one's life, but right from the beginning, and right from the moment one hears this, live life?

Meditation means an extraordinary activity of the brain, not silencing the brain. When the brain is at its highest quality, full of energy, there is silence. Not the silence put together by thought, which is limited silence. In that silence that can come only when there is freedom, there is love and compassion with its intelligence. That intelligence is supreme. But there is no compassion or love if you are attached to some religious organization or belief in something. There must be complete freedom, and in that freedom there is a great, tremendous energy because there is an emptiness, not nothingness, emptiness. In that there is that which is beyond all time.

This is meditation. This is religion.

[17]

THAT WHICH IS TIMELESS

WHAT IS IT that one is seeking? I think it is very important to go into this because we are all saying we are seeking truth, love, and so on. How can you seek truth if your mind is not in order? Order is putting things where they belong, in their right place. When the mind is confused, uncertain, groping, unclear, wanting security, wanting something or other, that very desire, that very uncertainty, must inevitably create illusion, or a delusion to which you cling.

So one must go very carefully into what it is that human beings, you and I, are seeking. Is it that we want to be happy? Is it because we are so unhappy, miserable, in conflict, uncertain, neurotic, that we say, "Please tell us how to live a life in which there is happiness"? Is happiness the opposite of unhappiness? If you are unhappy, miserable, living in great pain and anxiety and suffering, you want the opposite of that: clarity, a sense of freedom, happiness, order. Is that what we are seeking? Please listen carefully. Is the opposite something totally different from its own opposite? Or does the opposite have its root in its own opposite? Man has *invented* the opposite. Not that there is not dark and light, woman and man, and all that, but psychologically, inwardly, the opposite that we want, which we seek, is the projection of *what is*. If I am unhappy, I want happiness. That is all I know. Caught in this unhappiness, the reaction is to have the other, happiness. That which I want is born out of what is actually going on. So the opposite has its root in *what actually is*. So the opposite has no meaning. What has meaning is what is. I do not know how to face what is, therefore I invent the opposite. If I know what to do with what is actually going on, then the opposite does not exist. So the understanding of *what is* is far more important than the pursuit of what should be, or the opposite of *what is*.

Why are we unhappy, miserable, quarreling, violent? Why are we like this? That is *what is*. If I know how to transform *what is*, then the whole problem is solved. Then I don't have to follow anybody. Then I am a light to myself. So is it possible to solve *what is* without wasting our energy in the battle of the opposites?

It is possible only when you have total energy, which is not wasted in conflict. When I am unhappy, I have a sense of great anxiety. That is *what is*. To go away from that is a wasting of energy. To understand *what actually is*, I must use all the energy that I have; then I can go beyond it.

Order is necessary in life. Order, as we said, means putting everything in its right place. But we do not know what the right place is. We only know disorder. There is disorder now: wars. Aren't you in disorder yourself, now, in daily life? Now, that is the fact, that is what is going on. And we want order. We think order is the opposite of that. That is, we establish a pattern of order out of disorder. We are disorderly in our conduct, in our thinking, in our behavior, in our outlook, and so on, and we think order is a blueprint of the opposite of *what is*. In bringing about order as a blueprint, there is always conflict. That is the contributory factor of disorder. Where there is conflict there is disorder, nationally, politically, religiously, in every direction.

So there is disorder. That is a fact. Now can you observe, be aware of that disorder? Not try to change it, not try to transform it, not try to suppress it, not say, "I must have order out of it," but just be totally aware of that disorder in your life. Then you will see that out of that disorder comes order, which is not the opposite.

Freedom from authority is absolutely necessary to find out if there is, or if there is not, ultimate truth. And freedom from belief of any kind is necessary, which implies no fear, because belief exists where there is fear, where there is despair. And there must be order. These three things. Then we can proceed to find out what meditation is.

What is meditation? Why should one meditate at all? Is meditation something totally unrelated to daily living? Is meditation something you practice? Is meditation doing something that somebody says, the meditation of a particular system, a daily practice, a goal, an end to be achieved? You know what happens when you practice something over and over and over again; you become mechanical, your mind becomes dull, insensitive. Obviously. Isn't it so?

We think meditation is a process by which we can attain understanding, enlightenment, something beyond man's thoughts. This is generally what we mean by meditation. Have you practiced meditation? Have you practiced learning to control thought? Have you ever gone into the question of who the controller is? Who is the controller that is controlling thought? Is the controller different from the controlled? Or the controller is the controlled? You divide the controller and the controlled; and the controller then controls, tries to hold thought in a particular direction. But is the thought that wanders off different from the entity that is trying to control that thought? Aren't they both thought?

Meditation is to understand the proper place where thought belongs. Without control. Have you ever tried to live daily life without a single control? When you go into this question of meditation, you have to understand why man has developed this sense of controlling everything, controlling his thoughts, his desires, his pursuits. Why? And part of that is concentration. You know what happens when you concentrate; you build a wall of resistance within which you say, "I must concentrate on this," and therefore push everything else aside. Which is to exercise will to hold thought in a particular direction. And will is the expression, the essence of desire. And in concentration there is conflict going on. Your thought wanders off, all over the place, and you bring it back, and keep up this game. You have never asked why thought should be controlled at all. The mind chatters endlessly. If you have an insight, if you see where thought belongs, then there is no problem of control of thought.

As there is no system, no practice, no control of thought, then you have to find out what it means to be attentive. What does it mean to attend? Attention implies an observation without the center. The center is the "me," my desire, my fulfilment, my anxiety. When you are attending, which means giving your nerves, your eyes, your ears, everything you have with total energy, in that attention there is no center as "me."

Now, just experiment with what is being said. Are you attending now? That is, are you listening completely? Listen! That means not interpreting, not translating, not trying to understand what is being said, but the act of total listening. If you are, there is only that sense of hearing without a single movement of thought.

You cannot go to a school to learn it. You cannot go to a college or university to become sensitive, can you? You find out in your daily life whether you are sensitive or not by observing, by seeing how you react to people. So, attention is necessary. And that is part of meditation.

Meditation also implies a mind that is totally quiet—not enforced quietness, because in that then there is conflict, isn't there? The mind is chattering, thinking, listening, going on; but you can see for yourself that a mind that is completely still can really observe. If you want to look at mountains, with their shadows, with their light, with their beauty and their depth, then you look, *totally*. When your mind goes off, that is inattention. But when you want to see something totally, completely, your mind naturally becomes quiet, doesn't it? So for a mind that is inquiring into something that is not put together by thought, there must be this total attention, and therefore complete silence, quietness.

Most of us find it terribly difficult, because physically we are never quiet; we are always doing something with our hands, with our feet, with our eyes. There is always something happening. We are never aware of our own body. If you are, then you will find that it has its own intelligence, not dictated by taste, by the tongue, by the imposed artificial desire for tobacco, for alcohol and drugs. A mind that is inquiring into reality, into truth, has to be totally free from authority, from all belief. That is complete order! A mind that is endlessly chattering, endlessly analyzing, endlessly inquiring, is wasting its energy; but a mind that is completely still regenerates itself.

As we said, meditation is to have a completely still mind, and it can only be still naturally, not be a cultivated stillness, a practiced stillness. If you practice stillness, it is death, it is no longer stillness. You have to come upon it. You cannot have stillness of mind if there is no compassion. So we have to go into the whole question of what love is. Is love pleasure? Is it desire? Can a person who is ambitious love? Can a man who is competitive love? Can a man or a woman love when he or she is self-centered? Or is love when the self is not? When I am "me" with all my problems, with my ambitions, with my greed, with my envy, with my desire to fulfil, to become something, or imagining that I am a great man, as long as I am concerned about myself, love cannot exist. Love implies complete compassion.

Out of that comes complete stillness of mind, because the mind has put everything in its right place, put everything where it belongs, so it establishes right relationship between man and woman, a relationship that is not based on images, memories, hurts. Out of that comes complete attention and silence.

And what is that silence? What takes place in that silence? Can it be verbalized? That silence is not a gap when there is no noise. A silence when there is no noise is not silence, like having peace between two wars is not peace.

Suppose you have that exquisite, that extraordinary sense of the beauty of silence. What takes place when the mind is completely and totally silent? There is no movement of thought as time. There is no movement of thought as measurement.

Now I am going to say something that perhaps you will not like at all, because you are all very respectable people. When that silence takes place, there is space and absolutely nothing. There is space and absolutely nothing. See why it is important, because it is important to be nothing. Do you understand what I am saying? You are all somebodies. You all want to be something, either professionally, or you have delusions of grandeur; you want to achieve something or become something, realize something, fulfil. Which is all respectability. We are saying that in total silence, there is nothing, you are nothing. If you are something there is no silence, there is noise; and when there is noise you cannot hear or see. When there is nothing, there is complete stability. It is only when the mind is nothing that there is complete security, complete stability.

Only then can the mind find out if there is, or if there is not, something that is nameless, something that is beyond time. One has to live a life daily in which relationship with another has no conflict in it, because all relationship is life. If you do not know how to have a relationship with another without conflict, then life becomes distorted, ugly, painful, unreal.

All this is meditation. It is only then one comes upon that which is timeless.

ISBN 978-986-86215-34　　　　版權所有・翻印必究

大喆文庫 1

跨越時空的覺知：克氏首度公開發表的演講錄
The Pocket Krishnamurti

作　　　者	克里希納穆提（Jiddu Krishnamurti）	
譯　　　者	陳召強	
總 編 輯	劉秋鳳	
行　　　銷	徐千晴	
美術編輯	周曉佳	
出 版 者	親哲文化有限公司	
地　　　址	臺北縣235中和市中正路90號	
電　　　話	02-2247-5285	
傳　　　真	02-8245-5626	
E - M a i l	bright.discvry@msa.hinet.net	
B l o g	http://www.udn.com/ dos006	
總 經 銷	大和書報圖書股份有限公司	
電　　　話	02-8990-2588	
製版印刷	中原造像股份有限公司	
初　　　版	中華民國九十九年十一月	
定　　　價	三五〇元	

國家圖書館出版品預行編目資料

跨越時空的覺知：克氏首度公開發表的演講錄
克里希納穆提（Jiddu Krishnamurti）作·陳召強 譯
初版·新北市—中和市·親哲文化, 民99.11

譯自：The pocket krishnamurti
ISBN 978-986-86215-3-4（平裝）

1.印度哲學　2.生活指導　3.冥想

137　　　　　　　　　　　　　　99018869

喆哲嚞 埑惁晢杚

形聲字。從口，折聲。

本義：聰明，有智慧。

哲，知也。
《說文》

哲，智也。
《爾雅》

濬哲文明，溫恭允塞。
《虞書·舜典》

哲夫成城，
哲婦傾城。
《詩經·大雅·瞻卬》

視之不明，是謂不哲。
《後漢紀·桓帝紀》